The Art of
MAKING MOSAICS

Contemporary Mosaics by Louisa Jenkins.

The Art of
MAKING MOSAICS

by

LOUISA JENKINS

AND

BARBARA MILLS

D. VAN NOSTRAND COMPANY, INC.

PRINCETON, NEW JERSEY

TORONTO   LONDON

NEW YORK

D. VAN NOSTRAND COMPANY, INC.
120 Alexander St., Princeton, New Jersey *(Principal office)*
257 Fourth Avenue, New York 10, New York

D. VAN NOSTRAND COMPANY, LTD.
358, Kensington High Street, London, W.14, England

D. VAN NOSTRAND COMPANY (Canada), LTD.
25 Hollinger Road, Toronto 16, Canada

PRINTED IN THE UNITED STATES OF AMERICA

Preface

The purpose of this book is not historical but to present basic techniques of the art of making mosaics for this, the 20th century, so that teachers, artists, and amateurs may know what tools and materials are necessary and how to construct a mosaic. Also included are suggestions for designs and projects suitable for mosaics.

A mosaic is the orderly arrangement of parts composed into a permanent unified whole. Trees, beehives, the human body, all nature itself may thus be defined as a kind of vast mosaic. In this book, however, we are concerned with mosaics as an art form, one which uses enduring materials such as stone, glass, or tile, set in cements or adhesives.

Some see a similarity between our time and the break-up of the Roman Empire (the time when mosaic was widely used). Today, as then, there seems to be a chaos caused by the whole breaking into disordered parts. Might not this be the reason so many people are discovering hours of peaceful satisfaction in reversing this process in a small way and, with their own hands, taking a multiplicity of pieces and permanently setting them into an ordered whole? Nothing seems to delight children more. Such childlike simplicity carries over into the adult world. Therefore, this book is for a large audience composed of art schools, artists, housewives, doctors, office workers, and all those who have felt the revolt against the machine age and the assembly line. It should also find receptive groups in veteran hospitals and other institutions where art therapy has been an important aid to recovery.

Each person attracted to this medium will soon discover new materials and new ways of combining them. The results are myriad and limited only by the imagination. The very unfamiliarity with this medium will cause a fresh approach, and the worker will soon find that stones cannot be manipulated like oil paint. He will be forced into the virtue of simplicity. What to leave out, how to simplify and strengthen, have always been the concern of the artist. In mosaic the artist is immediately aware that he cannot do otherwise than be direct. You cannot fashion a hair line with small cubes of stone.

The use of mosaic as decoration shows a wide range. Although it is utilized by professionals in public buildings, churches and hotels, the amateur can make mosaics for his own home and garden and thus find not only self-expression but an economical and enduring way of beautifying the home. Mosaic as an art medium is almost indestructible. Earthquakes and wars are its only enemies.

We have so many new bindings, glues, mortars, that ways are being discovered of using mosaic that were impossible to the ancient world. These materials encourage artists to experiment. This book is merely a beginning and will be completed by all the people who put their own ideas, along with glass or stone pieces, into a permanent arrangement.

HISTORICAL NOTE

The beginnings of mosaic are mysterious. Most authorities believe the earliest artists worked around Damascus, Cairo, and the Near East. In 1400 B.C., Ikhnaton built the city of Tell el-Amarna in Egypt. He had the capitals of his temple columns inlaid with fragments of gorgeously colored glass and the spaces between the tesserae were gilt. Floor mosaics spread with the development of the Roman Empire, and in the third century B.C. the King of Syracuse installed a mosaic floor on his boat! These ancient floor pieces had a light or white background. Later, at the rise of the Byzantine period, this background was changed to gold. Mosaicists were sent out from Constantinople, capital of the Byzantine Empire, to decorate entire church interiors with stories of the Bible and religious symbols. As church art, mosaic reached its highest development in the Byzantine period from the fourth to the fifteenth century after Christ.

After the fifteenth century mosaic art began to decline. This was due in part to the glass industry, which had so perfected its techniques that mosaic glass was available in hundreds of shades. Mosaicists then copied paintings and mosaics became overcomplicated. This overcomplication is illustrated by an incident which took place in the sixteenth century. Zuccati, a noted mosaicist, was appointed to execute a church mosaic in Venice. He finished the piece but was suspected of using paint in certain parts of the mosaic. The Venetian Senate was indignant and appointed a commission of artists as a jury. Titian, Veronese and Tintoretto verified the charge and Zuccati had to do his mosaic over.

The decline of mosaic which began in the 16th century was rapid and almost complete. Glass industries ceased manufacturing mosaic glass and they did not produce it again until 1865. Nevertheless, certain methods of laying mosaic have remained the same for centuries. The method of laying mosaic used in Rome today, as well as its traditional style, is basically the same as that used in the 1600's.

LOUISA JENKINS
BARBARA MILLS

Acknowledgments

First of all I am indebted to all the people who have asked questions about the art of making mosaics; without the help of their curiosity this book would not have been begun. And without the encouragement of the publisher and the ability of the co-author, my daughter, Barbara Mills, it would never have been finished.

I wish also to express my appreciation to Douglas Madsen for his assistance with the drawings, and to Ellen Janson for the correction and typing of the manuscript.

Many of the photographs used to illustrate this book are due to the generosity of the following and have been used with their permission:

George Cain; Walter Goodwin; James H. Reed; David Shore; Peter Jenkins; Julius Shulman; Henry Inn; Sister Mary Corita, I.H.M.; Frank R. Chow; Corwin Hansen; Rothschild, of Los Angeles; William F. Dohrmann; Peter A. Juley and Son; Madelyn Studio; Frashers' Fotos; Jay Risling; Sonya Noskowiak; Rudolph Burckhardt; John R. Kennedy; Ben Schnall; Marion Carnahan; Emmett Bright; Junius B. Bird, of the American Museum of Natural History.

LOUISA JENKINS

Contents

List of Illustrations

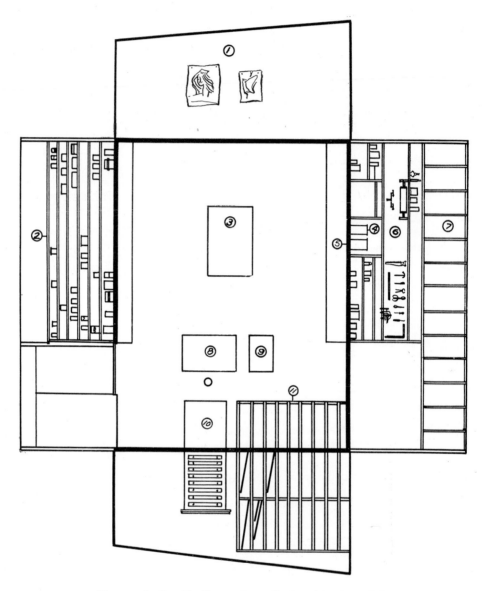

FIGURE 2. Studio floor plan. Scale ⅛ inch = 1 foot.
1. Pin up wall. 2. Tessera storage. 3. Mosaic table. 4. Magnesite.
5. Chloride solution. 6. Tools. 7. Windows. 8. Drafting table.
9. Roll table. 10. Chests for cartoons. 11. Storage.

1

The Workplace or Studio

For the beginner in mosaic who wants to make only a few pieces for his home, a complete studio is not necessary. He should, however, find a place close to a sink and one where his work will not be disturbed by the rest of the household. The cutting of glass and stone scatters chips. Also, cement and glue are messy materials. Some people find it pleasant to work in their gardens or patios if they are doing garden pieces. Yet outdoor work is limited by season. If no corner in the house is available, a part of the garage, preferably near a workbench, makes a fine partial studio.

Arranging a studio for a permanent workshop is a different matter. The size of this studio will depend on the amount of work to be carried on inside. Most commercial studios have started in one room and enlarged as their commissions multiplied. A lone artist will find a studio 20' x 26' adequate. Generally, however, if a mosaicist is asked if his studio is the right size, he will answer, "No . . . it should be a little larger. I don't really have enough room." This seems to be the answer whether the artist has rented a loft or a place which has the capacity of a hippodrome! Never does there seem to be enough space for all the materials, odds and ends collected by the artist. Old bits of wire, steel tubing, a stained glass window, lie about waiting for who knows what occasion.

Good lighting is essential in every studio. A roof skylight is best but often impossible to obtain. Windows which admit light from the north make excellent substitutes for a skylight. Northern light does not cast shadows as does that from the east, west, or south. Windows that allow the sun to shine directly upon a studio worktable should be furnished with blinds. A mosaicist will find it impossible to work with sunlight reflecting from the glass under his hands.

Artificial lighting has been so perfected that it can almost provide studio light in a closet. If a studio has only a few windows, lighting

1

fixtures should be located close to the ceiling. Select a strong, diffused light which does not cast shadows and has no glare. Fluorescent lights yield a workable light and are popular in the studio.

Most studios have four walls. The artist will find something to do with all of them, but a sliding type of garage door set into one wall facilitates moving large mosaics. A second wall should be left free for tacking up sketches and cartoons, which are the finished drawings made by a mosaicist. The best material for this wall is a porous compound called Cellotex.

A table approximately 4′ x 6′ will be necessary in the studio. It is good to have this table on rollers so that it can be moved. Planks laid across carpenter's sawhorses may be substituted for the table. In large studios, where assistants are employed, several tables are necessary, or the workers may sit at individual tables. An architect's drafting table is convenient for drawing and can be used to construct small mosaics. In order to avoid long hours of standing, a stool with a seat that can be raised and lowered is helpful. The studio should also have a sink with overhead shelves. Near this sink it is well to place a damp-proof garbage can, to hold magnesite or cement. Near this can should be a container for magnesium chloride, which will be mixed with the magnesite. A stone crock is essential for holding the chloride mixture, as chloride will erode any other material.

Shelves for storing glass and stone can be built along one wall. The glass and stone themselves may be kept in glass jars, shoe boxes, or aluminum pie plates. European studios often have numbered bins built into a wall. The Vatican workshop, which keeps on hand an enormous supply of different shades of glass, has long corridors of steel cabinets containing labeled drawers.

If a studio is spacious enough, it is well to have one corner where drawing and designing can proceed undisturbed by the actual laying of mosaic. In this corner it is convenient to keep a roll of wrapping paper for cartoons, in a rack such as meat markets use. This rack makes it easier to handle the heavy roll.

A workbench for making bases and bindings is an asset in any mosaic studio. If there is no room for a workbench, construction may be done on the studio table. In this case, reserve a space on the wall to hang tools. The good craftsman loves and respects his tools; he will take care to arrange them compactly in a rack where they cannot be damaged.

These suggestions are basic for every studio. However, studios are personal things. What seems chaos and disorder to one artist is a compatible workplace to another. The conclusion is obvious: each artist must finally fit into his own little cubicle or expand into a warehouse, according to his desires, aims, and the mosaic work involved.

FIGURE 3. Mosaic studio of Louisa Jenkins, Big Sur, California.

2

Materials Used in Construction

Mosaic materials are often called tesserae. Tessera (pl. tesserae) is a technical word used by mosaicists to denote the cut decorative material of which a mosaic is composed. Mosaic materials are so varied in scope that a beginner is likely to be bewildered at the array. He is also fascinated. Any artist who has watched adults as well as children enter a studio where tables are spread with multi-colored trays of stone and glass can testify to the attraction of these materials. Baubles of glass, clinking stones, and bits of bright crystal seem to fill a hunger in people. To handle them is happiness. From this wealth of material a beginner must finally choose his own. If he is indecisive, he need not become discouraged. Perhaps he may first be guided by the cost and availability of materials. Also, he might remember that natural earth colors organize well together, as opposed to a mosaic made entirely of materials in more vivid colors.

The commonest mosaic materials were once quite rare. In the first century after Christ, marbles and limestone were used almost exclusively in mosaic. These stones were imported primarily from Italy, and their color range was dull and limited. During the Augustinian period (28 B.C.–A.D. 14), cubes of glass enamel were manufactured. These cubes had few color tones—reds and other earth shades. Approximately two centuries later, gilt cubes, imported from Egypt, were included in the Roman baths of Caraculla. The rich use of stone and glass characteristic of Christian mosaics began at the time of Constantine the Great (A.D. 306–337). Glass mosaics were then carried eastward to India by the Saracens, who were Moslems, and westward to Europe by the Christian peoples. Thus two different religions were responsible for popularizing mosaic throughout the Western and Near Eastern world.

An examination of mosaic materials traditionally used, as well as those which have modern interest, will help the beginner in mosaic

4

to discriminate. Depending on their source, these materials may be divided into two general categories: manufactured and natural.

FIGURE 4. Basic materials.

MANUFACTURED MATERIALS

Tile

Tiles, the humble household variety, are known to every mosaicist. They often compose part of his work and have one advantage over other manufactured materials. Tiles are cheap and are an excellent source of supply for the beginner in mosaic.

There are two kinds of tile: ceramic and encaustic. Ceramic tiles are glazed and come in many shades and colors. Since a glaze is put on raw clay and then baked, these tiles are not a solid color all the way through. Encaustic tiles have color mixed and baked into their clay; hence, their coloring is solid. They are dull in finish, however, and possess a limited color range. Encaustic tiles are used commercially in floors. Because they come in sizes suitable for floors, the mosaicist will find it necessary to cut them.

Homemade ceramic tesserae provide a most inexpensive source of mosaic material. These homemade tesserae are especially adaptable for large-scale projects for schools and groups where making material is a rewarding and necessary part of making mosaics. However, the individual making a small mosaic will do better to purchase ceramic tesserae at a tile store; otherwise, it is essential to have a kiln for firing them. Some tile stores give away scraps of clay tile which may be cut and used for tesserae—an excellent way to obtain them. Used clay tiles, often discarded when buildings are torn down, may be taken to a tile store and sawed into strips convenient for nipping into tesserae as the mosaicist works.

The following process for making ceramic tesserae was developed by Sister Magdalen Mary, I.H.M., Chairman of the Art Department at Immaculate Heart College, in Los Angeles, California.

To make ceramic tesserae: Place a slab of clay on a table and roll it out (a rolling pin will do), much like cookie dough, to the thickness of the tesserae desired (Figure 5). The thickness of an ordinary ruler is good for most tesserae. A covering of paper, oilcloth or other thin material over the upper and lower surfaces of the clay will prevent it from sticking to the table and rolling pin. After the clay has been rolled out, it may be glazed immediately or several days later. When glazing is delayed, however, the clay should be kept damp and dried in a slow oven or by natural means just before glaze is applied. Glaze must be absorbed and will not adhere easily to damp clay. (After the slabs have been glazed, they may be stored on top of each other with a piece of plain paper between each slab. This paper protects the surface of the glaze.) The making and mixing of glazes is too intricate a process to be attempted without experience, so unless the person making tesserae is a skilled ceramicist, it is best to use commercially prepared glazes such as those found in a hobby shop. Glazes vary according to variations in clay. Accordingly, it saves time and effort to select glazes when purchasing clay to make tesserae. Commercial glazes come in many colors and are easy to handle. Apply glaze to the clay with a brush (Figure 6). When glazing, make sure the slabs lie flat so the tesserae will not have warped tops which reflect light distractingly.

It takes experience to determine when glazed slabs are ready for cutting into pieces (Figure 7). If a slab is too wet, it is hard to pick up the tesserae; if it is too dry, the pieces chip and the glaze falls off. When a slab is glazed as soon as it is rolled out, the clay should be solid enough to cut in from one to two hours. Avoid making a bevel, because edges which slant cannot be fitted close to each other. Cut tesserae into

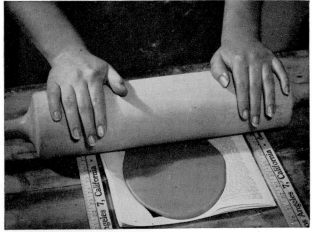

FIGURE 5. Roll out the clay.

FIGURE 6. Glaze the clay while it is still wet.

FIGURE 7. Cut the clay before it becomes leather hard.

MAKING OF CLAY TILE

various shapes: small and large, square and triangular, long and narrow. These tesserae must then be air-dried in a warm room, oven or sunlight, until the clay is dry. If tesserae are fired without air-drying, moisture inside the clay may create steam and cause the clay to explode.

Firing temperatures naturally depend on the glaze and the color desired. Generally speaking, commercial glazes are fired at a temperature around 1840° Fahrenheit or Cone 06. In a one-fire process, some glazes will crawl but they can be used for texture or may be refired with a touch of different colored glaze on exposed spots. Crackled glazes also add variety.

Glass

Glass is the material most commonly associated with mosaic. Indeed, glass is the staple of the mosaicist's art. Until recently, mosaic glass was manufactured in only one country—Italy. The trade name for this traditional glass is Smalti. Its manufacturing process is still a jealously guarded secret, handed down from family to family. Visitors to a glass factory are seldom allowed inside the rooms where mixing and firing take place. Since the import duty on Smalti is high, it is an expensive material to use. It is sold by the pound. However, there is no substitute for Smalti. This glass splits somewhat unevenly, giving it the much-prized reflective value possessed by all true mosaics. In comparison to Smalti, other types of glass lack depth and richness.

FIGURE 8. Cutting Smalti at Ugo Dona factory,
Morano, Italy.

In large architectural pieces, both for indoors and outdoors, Smalti is the superior material to use.

Smalti comes in hundreds of shades so that the slightest color gradations are available. It is manufactured in big pancakes and cut by machines at the factory (Figure 8). Generally it is cut into rectangles ½″ x ⅜″, although it is sold in other sizes. It may also be cut to order. However, since Italian manufacturers do not like to bother with small orders of Smalti, it is better to seek other sources of material unless one has a project of some scale. Because of recent demand, many tile dealers in America now stock Smalti.

Another mosaic glass manufactured in Italy and also in Mexico is known as Vitrious. This glass is used commercially in Italy. The United States imports it for store fronts, kitchens, and other practical decorations. Vitrious colors, while limited in scale, include some very brilliant ones. The glass itself comes in ¾″ squares, glued to paper in sheets one foot square. It is sold by the square foot. To remove the paper backing from Vitrious, soak it in water until loosened. The glass can easily be cut with tile nippers and is excellent when a project requires narrow strips of material. Vitrious is a thinner glass than Smalti. Its composition and reflective value are much inferior.

Stained glass is not restricted to windows but is often appropriated by the mosaicist. This material can be bought at any stained glass studio—most large cities have at least one. Studios often sell scrap material, left over when orders of glass have been cut; such material may be bought at a reduction. Stained glass is made in a wide variety of colors and surface textures, the most beautiful ones being manufactured in Europe. The brilliant color of stained glass results from light which passes through it. Of course it is not possible for light to pass through mosaic, since the tesserae are set in mortar. Consequently, a mosaicist must back stained glass with some reflective substance, such as aluminum leaf or gold paint.

Besides translucent stained glass, there are opaque types which are marbled in effect. Little used today, these opaque glasses are found when old churches or houses are torn down and their windows offered for sale. Such old glass, unexcelled in quality, is a great prize to find.

The ordinary mirror is another glass the mosaicist can use in modest quantities. No longer need one moan about seven years' bad luck! When a mirror is broken, pick up the pieces and know they will be used to advantage.

NATURAL MATERIALS

Pebbles

Nature produces a seemingly endless list of materials for the mosaicist. To begin with, pebbles are found in many places: beaches,
rivers, on the shores of lakes. They are used mostly in mosaics for
outdoor patios and walks. Because different localities produce different kinds of pebbles, they are fun to gather. Pebbles must be sorted
first into colors and then into sizes before they can be used effectively.
In garden mosaics the size of pebbles may range from that of a pea
to huge cobblestones, depending on the area to be covered.

Marble

Marble varies in hardness and may be purchased from the scrap
piles of any marble works. Scrap marble is best because it saves considerable cutting if bought in thin slabs. As a rule marble can be cut
in cubes but sometimes it is too soft and may crumble.

Cutting marble is a rather tedious process, but it is so individual
a material and comes in such delicate tones that the work is often
worth while. For this reason it is best to use marble in large-sized
cubes.

Crystals and Minerals

Crystals and minerals provide a field comparatively unexplored by
the mosaicist. Here artist vies with "rock hound," who also hunts
these treasures for his collections. On deserts, along the highways, near
beaches, there can be found many shops which specialize in crystals
and minerals. Sometimes one of these "shops" may be nothing more
than a shabby trailer, but such vehicles, unpromising as they may seem,
can present for sale the most exquisite specimens. When buying materials from a rock shop, ask if there are scrap pieces available. Again,
scrap has the virtue of being cheaper and often comes already broken
into small pieces. A mosaicist may find that certain materials, because
of their rarity, are too expensive for his art. Other materials are too
hard to cut. It is always advisable to inquire about the hardness of
materials before buying; this saves collecting too many attractive but
useless specimens.

Some crystals and minerals can be used more successfully than others. To aid the beginner, a partial list is given below. These materials

have all been tried successfully, but each person who is experimenting will find many more.

Quartz may be cut without difficulty along its <u>lines of cleavage</u>. This crystal comes in many shades: colorless, white, smoky, rose, violet, brown. These colors are both translucent and opaque. Rose quartz is especially valued for its glowing and subtle tint, but it is rarer than the colorless rock crystals.

Chrysocolla from Arizona is a vivid blue-green mineral used by the Indians in their cheaper turquoise jewelry. It is easily cut and has a blue difficult to match in any other material.

Sulphur crystal is imported from Sicily. As a rule it is too soft a material for mosaic but occasionally a few hard crystals can be purchased. These crystals have a pale yellow color with an unique appeal.

Amethyst is expensive, but it can be used with other materials in small quantities. It comes in hues from pale to dark violet.

Azurite is formed in nodules which can be cut. These nodules are solid in color, and their pale blue verges on violet.

Pyrites are too hard to cut but sometimes they can be bought as scrap material and used very interestingly. They are of a pale yellow color.

Selenite comes from Arizona and is especially good in mosaic. It is translucent and colorless and can be split into thin slices. The Indians of Arizona once used selenite for their window glass.

Lava is a beautiful gray-black or brown material. It is dull and, as background in mosaic, has interesting texture. This mineral can be found in the Arizona region, California, and many other places throughout the United States.

Asbestos in its natural state splits into long, thin, gray sticks and is a striking addition to certain areas of mosaic.

Iridescent furnace slag splits easily and can be purchased in black and green.

Agates and *jadeite* may be bought or found along beaches in pieces suitable for mosaic. They are smooth, water-worn stones which come in varied colors. Use them in specialized areas of mosaic. They are extremely hard to cut.

✳ Not so. Quartz has *No* cleavage. It will however fracture with a lovely fan-shaped concoidal pattern. Watch out - splinters are needle sharp!

3

Wood Base

Before assembling a mosaic, there must be something to assemble the mosaic on. A mosaic base is needed, either portable or fixed in place. Mosaics are the most permanent decoration known to man, and so their materials must be permanent. This includes the mosaic base. If a base is fragile or improperly constructed, it will not hold the mosaic stones in place over a long period of time.

A mosaic base of wood should never be used outdoors where the elements cause it to decay, but it can be waterproofed and made permanent enough for indoor pieces. While requiring some carpentry, a wood mosaic base is not difficult to construct. Its construction follows definite steps which anyone can master. The tools necessary to make a mosaic base are few, and most mosaicists prefer making their own bases for small-scale work. Bases for large-scale work can also be made in the studio if they are divided into sections.

PORTABLE TYPE

The most common base for a portable indoor mosaic is plywood. Although plywood is not the only material used for such a base, its results have been tested and are consistently good. However, in addition to plywood, there are many composition boards on the market. A composition board is one composed of various materials fabricated in sheet form. Industrial by-products, wood pulp, cane fiber pulp, cement and asbestos are some of the materials found in composition boards. These materials are pressed together and often mixed with a glue. Some composition boards make suitable mosaic bases, but they should be selected with care. Many of them will be too thin, too soft, or too porous. Boards which bend are impossible to use except for mosaics under one square foot. All composition boards should be tested for warping before they are used to make a mosaic base.

12

To construct a plywood or composition board base, the following equipment will be needed:

Materials: waterproof plywood or composition board, waterseal, brass binding, brass nails, galvanized window screening, staples, hangers, and screws.

Tools: brush to apply waterseal, anvil, hammer, electric drill or awl, pliers, tin shears, soldering iron, stapler, screw driver, ruler.

Waterproof plywood or composition board should be used, since non-waterproof board might warp with moisture and cause a split in the finished mosaic. The thickness of a base varies with the mosaic dimensions. For small mosaics, under 2 square feet, $\frac{1}{2}$ inch plywood is adequate. Average-sized mosaics, from 2 to 16 square feet, will require $\frac{5}{8}$ inch material. For all mosaics over 16 square feet, it is best to use a $\frac{3}{4}$ inch board. Plywood or composition board can be cut to specification when purchased at a lumber yard. Usually it is most convenient to have the yard do the cutting, since they have power saws and charge only a small fee for this service. However, plywood and composition board can be bought in standard-sized sheets 4' x 8'.

To further insure a base board against warping when it receives the wet mortar, apply two coats of waterproofing. A quick-drying type of seal will permit two applications during one working period. Allow the prime coat of waterseal to dry for one hour before applying the second. After the second coat has been given, allow the board to stand overnight. Be sure the edges and all sides of the board are sealed.

The mosaic base itself is constructed as follows, according to steps shown in constructing a hypothetical base board 18" x 24" (Figure 9).

1. Cut a piece of plywood or composition board of the desired size, in this case 18" x 24" (Figure 9-A). When cutting base boards to specification, a board should not be larger than 3' x 5' or the finished mosaic will be too weighty to handle. A base board larger than 3' x 5' should be divided into sections. The joinings of these sections will remain unobtrusive if a board is cut to follow the general divisions of the mosaic design. These sections can then be temporarily bound with wood. After the mosaic is completed, remove the wood strips, unless the piece is to be shipped. Wood strips will protect the mosaic's edge during transportation, and they can easily be removed when the work is installed.

2. Screw heavy-duty hangers to the back of the base board (Figure 9-B). Heavy-duty hangers are preferable to screw eyes, as they permit

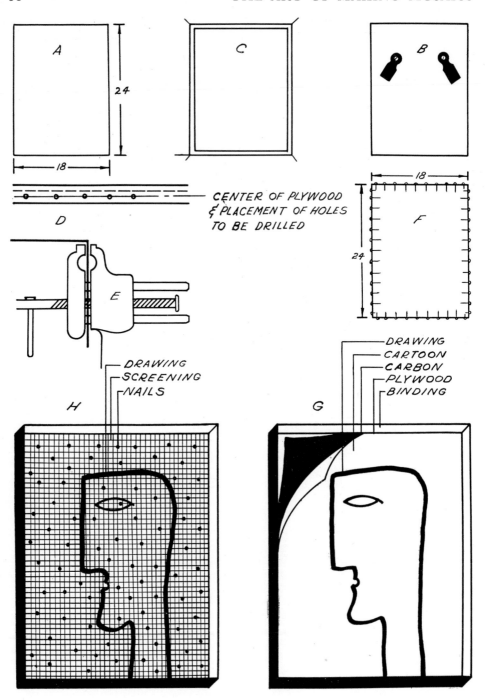

FIGURE 9. Construction of portable wood base.

the mosaic to hang flat against a wall. Portable mosaics usually require only two hangers, although large-scale portable mosaics may require more. These hangers are the same as those used to hold mirrors in place. They may be bought at any commercial glass store. Hangers must always be screwed into the base board before mosaic is laid. Otherwise, the screws might pierce a piece of finished work, causing it to crack.

3. Cut a length of metal binding equal to the perimeter of the base board plus 2 inches; i.e. 2 x (18″ x 24″) + 2″ = 86″. Make four marks on the metal strip, corresponding to the four corners of the base board (Figure 9-C). An extra 2 inches is allowed to compensate for loss in bending corners or inexactness in measuring. This metal strip should be approximately $\frac{1}{4}$ inch wider than the board. By protruding over and above the base board, it provides a bed into which the mosaic is laid.

Brass is a fine metal for binding, but aluminum, copper, or iron may be used. Binding material must be selected with two things in mind. The metal should harmonize with the decor of the room where the mosaic will hang. Also, the general color of the mosaic itself will indicate a choice of material.

4. Lay the metal binding flat on a table. With a grease pencil make the following nailing pattern on the binding: Measuring from the bottom of the metal strip, draw a line for nailing, equal to $\frac{1}{2}$ the thickness of the base board; i.e. $\frac{5}{16}$ inch. Mark places for nails 1 inch from corners. Divide the remaining spaces equally so that nails are approximately 2 inches apart (Figure 9-D). Drill nail holes. When thin binding metals are used, an awl and hammer will be sufficient to make these holes. Heavy metals will require an electric drill. Before using an electric drill, make indentations with a hammer and nail on the marks where the nails will be placed. This will prevent the electric drill from slipping off the metal binding.

5. Using a hammer and anvil, make four right angles in the metal strip (Figure 9-E). These angles correspond to the four corners of the base board. Tap the metal gently with a hammer to bend the right angle. The binding will now form a rectangle 18″ x 24″.

6. Fit the rectangular binding around the base board and nail it in place with $\frac{5}{8}$ inch brass tacks (Figure 9-F).

7. Cut off excess binding so that the two metal ends meet exactly. File these ends smooth or join them to make a neat joint.

8. After the base board has been bound, make an elementary reproduction of the cartoon on the board (Figure 9-G). This reproduction is to help you maintain your design when working with mortar. Only essential guide lines should be drawn; detail will be confusing. To transfer a cartoon to a base board: Cover the board with carbon paper, black side down. Lay the cartoon on top of this and, using a pencil, draw over its outlines. Very heavy cartoon paper may not permit an impression. In this case, trace the cartoon on thin paper and then transfer it to the board using the carbon paper.

9. Cover any portable mosaic base more than one square foot with a piece of galvanized window screening (Figure 9-H). Mosaics less than one square foot will not require screening. Cut the screening to fit the base board. Secure it to the board with brads or heavy staples. Fasten the screen from its center outwards so it will lie flat against the board. This will prevent raised surfaces which later might interfere with laying mortar.

FIXED-IN-PLACE TYPE

Wood bases for mosaics fixed in place are constructed in sections like portable mosaics. There are, however, two general methods of preparing a mosaic which is fixed in place for installation. The method chosen depends on the type of fastener used to keep the mosaic in place. This fastener, in turn, is determined by the construction and material of the place where the mosaic will hang. For instance, brick walls, because they crumble more easily, will require a different type of fastener from that used in a concrete wall. There are bolts and fasteners to fit every kind of surface or construction, but the following bolts are most commonly used to install mosaics.

Toggle bolts are made for construction which is hollow, such as a plaster wall. The bolt itself has a swing joint which slips into a hole and then is straightened perpendicular to the bolt and across the hole. The bolt is tightened, pressing the swing joint against the interior of the wall.

Expansion bolts are generally used in masonry or concrete construction. The bolt has a shank which swells as it is screwed into place.

Lag bolts which screw into expansion shields are also used for masonry or concrete construction. The shield expands as the bolt is screwed into it.

Keyhole bolts and shields are best for wood construction, though they may be used in concrete. The bolt is fixed in a structure, the keyhole shield screwed on the mosaic baseboard, and the shield attached to the mosaic is slipped over the bolt.

Power-driven bolts forced into a structure with an explosive are used for concrete and other solid-type masonry construction. These bolts have many trade names. Like cartridges, they are "shot" into a structure by means of an impact hammer detonated with explosive.

The first method of preparing a mosaic to be bolted in place works particularly well with toggle, expansion, or lag bolts. In this method, four holes are drilled in the four corners of the mosaic base board. These holes should be slightly larger than the bolts to be used. The holes should not be covered with mosaic. They must be patched with matching tesserae and tilesetter's glue after the mosaic is bolted in place.

The second method of preparing a mosaic to be fixed in place is better with keyhole bolts. No patching is necessary in this process. Four holes are drilled in the four corners of the mosaic base board. These holes are drilled on the back of the base board and do not penetrate all the way through. The holes should be shaped like a keyhole shield but slightly larger than the keyhole bolt head. The keyhole shields are then screwed over these holes. When the keyhole bolts are fixed into the surface, the mosaic is lifted and the shields slipped over the bolts, much as a man would hang his hat over a nail.

4

Concrete Bases

Concrete is a mixture of Portland cement, coarse aggregate, fine aggregate, and water. Sooner or later the artist who makes both indoor and outdoor mosaics in quantity will consider using concrete as a base. Just as, in the kitchen, bread is termed "the staff of life," so concrete might be called the mason's "staff." This is true for many reasons. Concrete, especially when used in large masses, is an economical material. It is also one of the strongest and most permanent materials known. A base made of concrete may be shaped into an interesting free form, an effect more difficult to achieve with wood. Moreover, for the mosaicist, concrete becomes both base and mortar, combining two processes —the construction of base and the mixing of mortar—into one. Finally, concrete can be reinforced to carry huge loads, and a mosaic spread over a wide area is often very heavy.

Concrete bases, like concrete mortars, are sensitive to temperature. They should always be mixed in temperatures above 50°F. Allow concrete to dry or cure slowly in temperatures above 32°F. During this period, sprinkle with water or cover it with wet cloths. Concrete slabs should be kept moist for approximately seven days.

PORTABLE TYPE

A portable base slab made of concrete is more commonly used in Europe than in the United States. Such bases are excellent when mosaic is exposed to the elements. However, they have the disadvantage of being weighty. Portable concrete base slabs should not be made for mosaics more than 3 square feet or they will lose much of their portability. When a larger portable concrete base is needed, it must be divided and constructed in sections, then reassembled later in the same manner as a portable wood base (Figure 10).

18

FIGURE 10. Division of large mosaics.

To make a portable concrete slab, the following tools and materials will be necessary:

Tools: saw, hammer, trowel, container for mixing concrete.
Materials: wax paper, form lumber, nails, Portland cement, sand, reinforcing material.

Portable concrete slabs can easily be constructed in the studio. Using 2″ x 4″ lumber or scrap boards, make a form the size of the base desired. This form should be not less than 2 inches deep. It may have a bottom or, more simply, may be placed on waxed paper to prevent the concrete from sticking to the supporting surface. A piece of expanded mesh or several steel rods are used to reinforce the slab. If expanded mesh is chosen, cut the mesh one inch smaller than the base. Place the mesh at mid-depth in the form. Make sure it is equally free from all edges of the form. The mesh can be wired in place or temporarily supported on rocks or other masonry material. Reinforcing rods come in round or square sections. If these are used, select $\frac{1}{4}$ or $\frac{3}{8}$ inch rods and place them at mid-depth in the form, maintaining the same clearances as for mesh. Place the rods 6 to 10 inches apart.

Mix concrete for a setting bed, using one part Portland cement to three parts sand. Coloring material, the double-strength, limeproof, sunfast type, should be blended with the dry cement, if desired. Add water until the mixture is the consistency of a very thick cake batter. The weight of the slab may be lightened somewhat by adding wood chips or packing-case excelsior up to 3% by weight, but this should be done carefully or too much extraneous material will cause the slab to crack. Ten percent aged lime putty or hydrated lime will make the concrete more workable. Plaster of Paris, added up to 2%, will delay its setting time.

Sizable areas of mosaic incorporated permanently into architecture are often set in a concrete slab. Pouring this slab then becomes a major operation. Unless an artist is very experienced in mixing concrete, it should not be attempted without a cement mixer and an assistant laborer. Pouring a concrete slab is also an operation which involves well-timed cooperation between artist and laborer. More concrete must not be poured than can be set with tesserae during one working period; otherwise the concrete will grow too hard for the tesserae to be embedded.

Concrete slabs for fixed-in-place mosaics are composed of two mixes: a rough bed and a setting bed. The rough bed contains coarse aggregate such as crushed rock. It is poured first. The setting bed, which must be of a smoother consistency, contains fine aggregate such as sand. It is best to pour a setting bed on top of the rough bed while the latter is still soft and wet. In this way the setting and rough beds together form integral parts of one concrete slab. If a setting bed is poured after the rough bed has become hard and dry, the slab is then composed of two layers rather than one. Furthermore, the setting bed becomes ineffective structurally and serves only to hold tesserae.

Concrete slabs for floors and patios must be at least four inches thick, reinforced with 6x6 10/10 steel mesh. This thickness is necessary because reinforcing must be placed 3 inches from the ground (rough bed) and covered by one inch of concrete (setting bed). For slab footings, waterproofing, and drainage details, a state building code should be consulted.

Forms to confine a patio or floor slab are made from 2" x 4" lumber. The ground within the form is then thoroughly soaked with water. A piece of 6x6 10/10 steel mesh is cut to the shape of the form but one inch less than its inside diameter. This mesh is laid on the ground, keeping its edges free of the form.

Mix, then, for the rough bed: one part cement, two parts sand, three or four parts aggregate. This mixture should be the consistency of ordinary cake batter, slightly more watery than the mixture for a setting bed. Pour this mix over the steel mesh to a depth of 3 inches if the setting bed is to be applied before the rough bed has hardened.

Then carefully pull the mesh upwards until it comes near the surface of the rough bed. For the setting bed, mix the concrete formula given for a portable concrete slab and pour this mixture over the mesh the remaining depth of one inch. Level the concrete slab by pulling a board over its form, and lay the tesserae.

When it is necessary to pour a setting bed of concrete after the rough bed has hardened and dried, the rough bed itself must cover the reinforcing material by one inch. Before applying a setting bed, soak this rough bed with water. Do not allow water to stand in pools on the slab, however. Just before the setting mixture is poured, slosh on the rough bed a mixture of cement and water the consistency of thin soup. This mix will provide a firm bond between rough and setting beds. An alternate mix for this purpose utilizes plastic cement glue. This glue is diluted half-strength with water, then mixed with cement until the whole is the consistency of thin soup. It is then sloshed on a rough bed of concrete that has previously been soaked with water.

There are two types of slabs which are poured flat and, after drying and being embedded with tesserae, are lifted into position with heavy equipment. These are known as tilt and lift slabs. They are of such proportion and weight that their reinforcing requires the services of an engineer.

Generally, when applying mosaic to an already standing masonry structure, such as a brick wall, it is not necessary to pour a rough bed of concrete. The wall itself serves as the rough bed. In every case, however, the wall must be carefully tested to determine whether it will support a mosaic. If the wall is sufficiently strong, it is wet down and roughened with a tool to insure a better bond. Then either the soupy mix of concrete is applied or a mix of plastic cement glue, water and cement, forming a bond between rough and setting beds. Finally a setting mixture of concrete is plastered over the wall and tesserae embedded in this mixture. A paste-like mortar of plastic cement glue, cement and water may be used to replace the setting bed, if desired. When this mortar is used, it is not necessary to apply soupy concrete mix to form a bond. The masonry surface is merely made wet and roughened with a tool.

FIGURE 11. Basic tools.

5

Preparation and Cutting of Materials

Cutting mosaic material is a mechanical process. Like many mechanical processes, whether it is tedious or pleasant depends primarily on one's attitude and ingenuity. Climate permitting, mosaic material can be cut outdoors. A worktable on wheels will facilitate the moving of material between studio and garden. If the mosaicist cuts tesserae outdoors, he may find himself combining sunbathing and bird-watching with his art. Music also lends itself well to such occasions. A good record library can be as important to the mosaicist as a good pair of tile nippers.

When a group of people are working together on a project, the hours of cutting material may be filled with conversation, much like an old-time sewing bee. Houseguests, who always seem curious about mosaics, can be pressed into service after a little practice. Taken altogether, the mosaicist should find the preparation of his material a satisfying process. If cutting tesserae sometimes produces a stiff back and arm, it also produces a sense of accomplishment that is lost to many people these days, the accomplishment of helping to create something beautiful with one's own hands.

The first rule to remember when cutting mosaic material concerns the size of the tesserae. Tessera size is determined by the size of the mosaic itself. If a mosaic is extensive and covers a wall, tesserae and stones several inches long can be used. However, if a mosaic is small, less than one square foot, it will require bits of material, some of them cut into pieces approximately $1/8$ inch in diameter. Chips from cutting material should always be saved; these are handy for small projects and specialized areas of mosaic.

TILE

Tools: tile nippers, pliers, (adjustable jaw cutnipper—optional).

The beginner in mosaic will find tile a comparatively soft material to cut. For this reason, the construction of a tile mosaic will encourage people who have had little experience in preparing material. Tile can sometimes be used without cutting, if a mosaic is large. Most often, however, the corners of tile must be nipped or the tile must be cut into simple shapes.

To cut tile, hold a tile nipper at right angles to a piece of material. Barely catch the tile's edge in the jaws of the nipper, squeeze, and bite

FIGURE 12. Cutting Smalti or tile.

through (Figure 12). Long-handled nippers facilitate the cutting process. Cutting tile will require some practice, but a beginner can soon do it without difficulty. As cutting proficiency develops, few shapes will be too complicated to form.

A tool which will benefit the professional mosaicist or serious amateur is an adjustable jaw cutnipper. It has expandable jaws and consequently can be regulated to cut tile, thick glass, and Smalti. An expensive tool, it can be bought only at large hardware shops. Nevertheless, the adjustable jaw cutnipper saves hours of labor and is worth its extra cost when there is considerable cutting to be done.

SMALTI

Tools: hardie, mosaic hammer or brick mason's hammer, eyeshield, tile nippers.

The best tools for cutting Italian Smalti are a hardie, set in a block of wood or log, and a mosaic hammer (Figure 13). An eyeshield should

FIGURE 13. Cutting marble on hardie.

always be worn when cutting Smalti; inexpensive plastic bubble eye-shields can be bought at most hardware stores. The hardie can be purchased wherever forges are sold or at junk yards, as it is part of an anvil. Imbed the hardie in wood. A tree log makes a good base for this tool because it can be cut to a comfortable height and then placed between the legs of a person sitting down. A sitting position seems to be the most comfortable when cutting Smalti. Remember to wear an eyeshield.

Mosaic hammers are manufactured only in Europe. In this country they can be made to order at a tool shop, or a brick mason's hammer can be substituted. The latter, while long in the blade, serves adequately. When selecting a hammer, choose a weight which is most comfortable to handle. This weight will vary with the individual, so that the most workable hammer is a matter of preference.

To cut Smalti, hold a piece of material at right angles to the hardie blade. Take a hammer and strike the glass with a quick light touch. This striking motion requires skill. A firm wrist is necessary or the glass will shatter, but if the wrist is too tense, it will tire after only a few strokes. The beginner should work with patience. Like learning a golf swing, the only way to learn how to cut Smalti is by practice. It will help the beginner to vary his cutting routine. When the wrist tires from preparing Smalti, cut another kind of material with tile nippers or use a glass cutter.

Marble and stone are also cut with a mosaic hammer on a hardie. Smalti may be cut with tile nippers, but when dealing with material over $\frac{1}{4}$ inch in thickness a hardie will save much time and labor.

GLASS

Stained glass loses its brilliance when laid in mortar. Consequently, before stained glass is cut, a shiny backing must be applied to reflect light. This brilliant backing is achieved in several ways. An easy method is to spray the glass with gold or silver paint. Such paint comes in convenient spray cans, may be applied quickly and dries in a few hours, but it does not give the highest brilliance. Gold, silver and aluminum leaf are the best materials used for backing glass. They yield a reflection, a beauty unequaled by any other backing material. While their application takes more time than does paint, it is impossible to find a substitute for their results.

APPLYING LEAF TO GLASS

Materials: egg set, metal leaf, brush, cotton or soft cloth.

The egg set used in applying leaf is the same as that used commercially to preserve eggs. It acts as an adhesive between the metal leaf and the glass. When used to hold leaf, this liquid should be diluted, one part egg set to six parts water. If egg set is difficult to locate, a gelatine solution for applying leaf may be obtained at most paint stores. Workmen who letter glass signs sometimes use gelatine, but egg set does the job very well.

Gold, silver, copper, and aluminum leaf come in paper books. Aluminum leaf is much to be preferred over the others. It is cheaper. Also, gold and silver leaf are so thin that they require great skill to manipulate. The slightest breath of air tears or destroys them. Aluminum leaf is thin but tougher, and it results in the same high brilliance.

The paper book containing aluminum leaf is 5½ inches square, each piece of leaf being protected by a sheet of tissue paper. Cut the back edge of this book. In this fashion, it is possible to remove separately each piece of leaf and its protecting tissue.

On a studio table lay out the glass to be leafed. If the glass is textured, be sure it is placed rough side up. Leaf is applied to a rough surface to save the smooth side for cutting. With a brush, cover the surface of the glass with egg set. Then, pick up a piece of aluminum leaf together with its sheet of protecting paper on top and lay it carefully on the glass. The leaf must be placed with precision. Aluminum and the wet liquid attract each other, so that once applied the leaf is hard to move. Furthermore, aluminum leaf is delicate material that may be spoiled by drafts or air currents. It is wise to keep all studio doors and windows closed when handling aluminum leaf.

CUTTING STAINED GLASS

Tools: glass cutter, felt or cloth pad, steel ruler, pliers, tack hammer.

Before cutting glass for mosaic, it is helpful to study a craftsman who cuts window glass. Such men seem to cut without pressure or effort. To watch an experienced stained glass craftsman (there are not many left) cut a curved shape to a pattern with ease and precision is a joy to behold! Such skill takes years to acquire.

The beginner should first cut glass in straight lines: squares, rectangles, and triangles. It will not be long before he develops confidence. Give due respect to the glass itself. Fingers may be cut severely if this material is handled without sufficient care. Never pick up glass by its edge. If a piece of glass does not break readily, hold it with pliers, not by hand. Cutting glass is such a delicate process that gloves can not be worn. They will only make the work awkward and sloppy.

To cut glass: Lay the material smooth side up on a felt or cloth-padded table (Figure 14). Laminated glass has only one side which is easily cut. Find this side by making a small mark on both sides of the glass with the glass cutter. The side which marks more easily is the one

Figure 14. Cutting glass.

to cut. The cutting tool itself usually has two parts: a cutting blade and a ball for tapping and breaking the glass. When ready to cut, draw the glass cutter across the glass with a sure, sharp sweep of the hand. For example, to cut a piece of glass into ½ inch squares, score it with the cutter into a series of lines ½ inch apart, parallel to each other, and then a series of lines ½ inch apart at right angles to the former lines. Then turn the glass over and tap it with the ball end of the glass cutter. This will break it into squares. Some imported glass is difficult to break. Tap this glass with a tack hammer and it should yield. When cutting very heavy glass, use a steel ruler to guide the wheel of the glass cutter.

After some practice in cutting straight lines, try curves by guiding the cutter against a cardboard pattern. Round pieces of glass are cut with tile nippers in the same manner as tile.

POUNDING AND SAVING OF SCRAPS

Tools: eyeshield, ball-headed hammer, cardboard, heavy screening, sieves.

Many crystals, lava, geodes, and, in certain instances glass are prepared by pounding into fragments. A solid foundation such as a cement floor or outside patio is necessary for this pounding. The safest place to work is outdoors, since chips fly off the material. To prevent these chips from scattering too widely, place a shield of cardboard or carton boxes around the pounding area. Cover the rock or crystal that is to be cut with a heavy wire mesh. This prevents pieces from flying in the artist's face. *Always wear an eyeshield when pounding material.*

When the material has been covered with mesh, pound it vigorously until it is well broken. Sweep up the material and put it into a fine sieve. Powder will strain through this sieve, leaving the pieces desired. When two grades of material are necessary, use two sizes of sieve. It is well to pound large amounts of material at one sitting. Save the different-sized fragments of material and store them in separate containers.

Some crystals have a cleavage along which they are easily broken by pounding with a hammer and chisel, as a sculptor does in chipping stone. Selenite, or mica as it is commonly called, can be split into thin sheets with a kitchen knife. These sheets can then be broken into pieces of any size.

6

Mortars

From earliest times people have sought to develop the perfect mortar. Cement seems to have met with immediate success. Roman peoples combined slaked lime and volcanic ash to produce a cement similar to what mosaicists use today. Their concrete was incredibly strong. For instance, many of the mosaic floors of the Caracalla Baths in Rome, made 1700 years ago, are still intact. Their tesserae, where not destroyed by earthquakes, have remained safely imbedded in concrete (Figure 15).

Cement mortar is still the most common kind used in mosaics. Today, however, mortars can be obtained in a variety of commercial mixes.

FIGURE 15. Floor mosaic, ruins of Caraculla Baths, Rome.

In every case, the type, size, and location of the mosaic itself should be considered before a mortar is selected.

READY-MADE CONCRETE MIXES

Two kinds of concrete mix can be bought ready-made. While these preparations come in 60 pound sacks and are convenient to use, they are too costly for mosaics larger than a few yards square. Of these, mortar mix is a combination of sand and cement to which aggregate and water must be added. Concrete mix contains cement, sand and crushed rock to which only water is added. Climate and the amount of water added to these mixes have a definite effect on their strength. The mixes themselves should not be stored more than a few months before use or they will form mortar that has a tendency to crumble.

NON-READY-MADE CONCRETE

When working on large-scale projects, such as patios or floors, it is best to prepare mortar on the job. Portland cement sold in 94-pound sacks will prove the cheapest cement mortar for these projects. Portland cement is sold in two shades: gray and white. Gray cement is used in most mortars, since a bright concrete background in mosaic is unusual, and colors added to gray cement, reds or blacks, for example, remain dull in tone. White cement is more expensive than gray, and its strength is somewhat weaker. It is used when brighter backgrounds are required. By adding color to white cement, the mosaicist is able to match background to tesserae.

The only kind of coloring materials which can be added to concrete and retain their hues are double-strength, limeproof, sunfast colors. These materials, which come in powder form, are manufactured specifically for coloring concrete. Color must always be added to dry cement. It is thoroughly blended with the cement powder and sand before the addition of water.

To pour the small area of concrete sufficient for such projects as a mosaic table top, bird bath, or door step, mix concrete for a rough bed: one part cement, two parts sand, three or four parts aggregate. Crushed stone makes the best aggregate. For the mosaic, setting-bed mortar is used: one part cement to three parts sand. To delay the setting time of both base and setting mixtures, 2% plaster of Paris may be added. Aged lime putty or hydrated lime added up to 10%

makes the concrete workable. These ingredients give the mixtures a fatter rather plastic consistency.

Another cement mix is grout. Grout is a substance of cream-like consistency used to fill cracks between tesserae. To make grout: add one part lime putty to five parts Portland cement. Color, if needed, should be blended with the dry cement powder. Water should then be added slowly until the mixture is about the consistency of cream. This thin grouting mix can be worked into cracks between the tesserae. It leaves a smooth surface.

MAGNESITE

Magnesite is a hard cement used in composition flooring. Although it cannot, except in an especial mix, be used for outdoor slabs, this material makes a very fine mosaic mortar, for three reasons. First, the setting time of magnesite can be somewhat controlled. Second, it is easier to handle than concrete. Third, magnesite forms a firm bond with a wood mosaic base, while the bond formed by concrete is likely to be less firm. However, since magnesite is sold only at major supply houses, it is sometimes more difficult to obtain than ready-made cements. It is also a rather complicated material to store and mix. Furthermore, magnesite, sold in no less than 100-pound sacks, is because of its very bulk unsuitable for the person who wants to make a single small mosaic. For these reasons, a beginner in mosaic might well select another mortar such as ready-made cement, a glue, or a mastic for his work.

Sacks of magnesite may be purchased from flooring dealers, but each store seems to have its own mix and the standards are not rigid. Asbestos fibers, silica, wood fibers and talc, some or all of these ingredients may be present in a magnesite mix. However, the one best suited for mosaics is labeled Sculptor Mix. This is an indoor, non-waterproof material. It is white and made to receive color. Magnesite is also available in an outdoor mix that is waterproof. This cement is impervious to weather and should always be used for mosaics that will be placed outside. It is gray in color but, because of the waterproofing chemical, dries blue. If a blue shade is undesirable, color may be added to the dry magnesite.

Magnesite, when used for mortar, is mixed with a strong solution of chloride. Chloride, either in solution or crystals, can be bought together with magnesite from a flooring contractor. The chloride solution, diluted to proper strength, comes in 5 gallon tins. Crystals are packed in 100-pound sacks. When using large quantities of magnesite, it is cheaper to buy crystals. Crystals also make it possible to control the density of the liquid mixed with magnesite, though they are harder to store. Chloride crystals should not be kept in the sack, as they have the property of extracting moisture from air and the sack will soon begin to leak. Both crystals and liquid chloride should be stored in a stone crock. They will erode any metal container.

To prepare a chloride solution from crystals, stir in just enough water to dissolve the chloride crystals. Float a heavy range 19-31 Baumé hydrometer in the liquid and add water until the hydrometer reads 25°. This solution, mixed with magnesite, will yield a quick-setting mortar. To make a mix which will set more slowly, add water until a minimum reading of 19° is obtained on the hydrometer. The more concentrated the solution of chloride, the stronger and more quick-setting a mass of mortar will result.

When mixing magnesite mortar, add color to the dry magnesite and blend thoroughly. Next, stir in chloride solution until the magnesite is the consistency desired. This consistency depends primarily on the preference and experience of the artist. Unlike other cement mortars, magnesite will form a strong mass when used either as a thick paste or when thinned to a creamy substance. Some artists find a stiff magnesite mass easier to control when setting stones; others will choose a thin mix. A stiff mix will be easier for the beginner to handle.

Exposure to magnesite and cement will cause sore, rough hands. Keep these substances off the skin as much as possible. Wash arms and hands frequently. Magnesite will also erode and pit tools; consequently, all tools should be washed after each day's work.

SPACKLE

Spackle is a patching plaster which comes in small packages. When the dimensions of a mosaic are small, spackle is a convenient mortar to use. It is, however, too expensive a material to buy in quantity. Spackle can be made weather resistant by adding one teaspoon of clear varnish to the dry mix. In this state it forms a compact tough mass called Swedish putty.

Because it is easy to control and not harmful to hands, spackle makes an excellent mortar for children to use.

GLUE

Many people prefer to set mosaic in glue. This material has the advantage of being a familiar one and it is applied without being mixed. However, glue is not as permanent a material as cement. The cracks between tesserae set in glue will be larger than those set in cement mortar.

Ancient peoples used glue for mosaics in many ways. In Peru, a gummy resin of tolu was used to set large Mochica ear ornaments. These ornaments have been dated approximately A.D. 400 to 1000. Recently, when some of these ear-pieces belonging to the Raphael Larco collection were being shipped to the Arts of the Andes exhibit at the Modern Art Museum in New York, a few fragments became loose, but the majority remained firmly in place. Peruvian tolu balsam is a gummy resin of low melting point and is soluble in acetone.

Christians of the 11th century liked to travel with mosaic panel ikons. Their ikons were composed of tiny tesserae held with a mixture of wax and resin. The wax-resin mix was spread directly on the wooden panel, where it was light and tough. This glue was also damp-proof.

Modern glues have a polyvinyl acetate resin which acts much like the resin in ancient Peru. However, the acetate resin of today has been strengthened and made water resistant. A mosaicist will find many polyvinyl acetate glues offered for sale under various trade names. All of these glues, sold at hardware stores, are suitable for mosaics where cement mortar is not desired.

Casein glues form another class of adhesives. They dry transparent but are milky in color when applied. They are less water resistant than polyvinyl acetate substances. When buying a casein glue, it is best to read its label and make sure the glue is water resistant.

Plastic cement glue is a new product. This glue is diluted half-strength with water and mixed with cement to form a paste-like mortar. Its chief advantage is that it can be applied directly on a rough bed of concrete, where it takes the place of a setting bed. It should be spread to a thickness slightly greater than the thickest tessera, and then the tesserae immediately embedded; or each tessera may be buttered with the paste and set into place. This cement glue is excellent when applying mosaic to vertical surfaces, but it is best when confined to masonry. It is more expensive to use plastic cement glue than to mix concrete for a setting bed, and this should be considered before a large project is begun.

Tile mastic is an organic adhesive manufactured especially for the installation of tile. This product is water resistant but highly inflammable. It sets more quickly than most mortars.

Transparent glues are found in various containers, such as bottle or tube. They are used when a base board is colored and when it is desirable to let color show through the adhesive.

7

The Direct Method

The direct method of laying mosaic is the one in which each tessera is placed by hand into a setting bed of mortar. This method of laying tesserae was used from early times until mosaic reached its peak in the 13th century. Only when mosaic art began to decline was a process of laying mosaics on paper invented for economic reasons. It became cheaper for artists to keep a group of workmen in their studios and to

FIGURE 16. Wall mosaic from Nea Moni Monastery, Island of Chios, Greece.

ship mosaic pre-assembled on paper rather than to send men away for long periods and support them on the job. Today, however, many new composition boards have been developed. These are both light and durable. On such boards even large-scale pieces done by the direct method can be made in the studio.

There are several key advantages to the direct method. Tesserae, when placed directly into mortar, cause an unevenness in the surface of the mosaic. This surface texture makes the work more alive. Movements on the part of the spectator change the angle of reflection, causing a shift in play of light. Through movement, the observer also becomes a participator. This phenomenon explains somewhat the tremendous power of early mosaics. However, such vitality is difficult to retain in any more mechanical method, where a smooth surface is the result. Smoothness, of course, is essential where mosaic is used in a utilitarian manner. Tables, floors, counters in kitchens or bathrooms, all are products of the "paper process" or reverse method. But where mosaic is used as decoration in the category of a fine art, rough texture and a primitive piece-by-piece approach give effects which can be achieved in no other way.

DIRECT METHOD USING ADHESIVE AND TITLE CEMENT

This method (Figure 17) is used when mosaic is constructed of tesserae having a uniform thickness. It is also a good one for children and amateurs because adhesive is easier to handle than magnesite or cement. An amateur is one who cultivates an art for love and not for profit. So if one wishes to do a simple piece for home or garden, this is the method to use. Preliminary work of designing the cartoon and constructing a base board are the same as in any other method. This operation, however, is simplified because no wire screen is necessary. One works directly on the base board.

To make a small decorative mosaic, cut a piece of plywood or composition board 8″ x 9″. This size adapts itself to a mosaic which will be useful about the house. The mosaic might be used on the dining table for a hot pad, set under a vase or flower arrangement, placed on the wall behind a candle. In the kitchen it could be fastened to cabinet doors, adding color to that important room.

The best material for beginners to use in making such a mosaic piece is either ceramic or encaustic tile. Venetian glass, however, has

FIGURE 17. Construction using tile cement, direct method.

more color than tile and makes a brighter square. If tesserae are to be cut according to a design, a tile nipper will be needed plus a spatula for spreading adhesive. Cut the material into squares approximately ¾ inch.

On a table, lay the base board together with a can of adhesive and the pieces. Then pick up the tesserae and freely arrange them on the base board. Try different colors and patterns. Shift the tesserae around, cutting them if necessary, until a pleasing design is achieved (Figure 17-A). Often it helps to mark colors on the board so that they are not forgotten when the board is cleared. When ready to glue tesserae to the board, butter each piece of material with adhesive. A small spatula is handy for this job. Another method of gluing is to spread each separate color section of the board with adhesive and lay tesserae down while the adhesive is wet (Figure 17-B). Since adhesive hardens within an hour, cover only as much of the board as can be completed in that time. The area covered will also depend on tile size; big squares naturally cover an area more quickly than small ones. Set the tesserae as close as possible if grouting is not desired. When a section of work is finished, cover it with a damp cloth to prevent it from drying too quickly. After the mosaic is set and dry it may be grouted (Figure 17-C). If grout is used, the work has a more finished appearance and a smoother surface; furthermore, tesserae do not have to be fitted together so exactly. The last step in making a decorative tile is to nail a strip of wood molding around the edges of the mosaic, to give the edges a finished appearance.

A variation of the adhesive method is just as successful. Paint a design directly on the board with oil or commercial paints. After several days, when the paint has thoroughly dried, set tesserae in the above method, using a glue which dries transparent. Casein glues are best for this purpose. When a design is painted directly on the base board, beautiful effects can be obtained by using partly opaque tile and squares of transparent stained or pebbled commercial glass.

GROUTING

Grouting is the spreading of mortar between cracks in mosaic tesserae. Ready-mixed grout in cans is available at tile supply houses; although, when dealing with a large mosaic, it is best to prepare grout in the studio. Grout is made by adding one part lime putty to five parts Portland cement. Color, if desired, is blended with the dry cement powder. When selecting color, choose a shade which will harmonize with the mosaic tesserae. For instance, if light tesserae are used, color the grout mixture a light gray or tan shade. When grout has been mixed to the consistency of cream, spread it over the mosaic and work it into all the cracks between the tesserae. Then remove the excess mortar with a spatula or squeegee. Let the mosaic dry for twenty-four hours. After the work is set and dry, turn it upside down and nail a stripping or half-round molding of wood around the edges of the base board. Make sure this stripping is flush with the tesserae (Figure 17-D). Now the mosaic is ready to clean. Try soap, water and a knife to remove specks of adhesive. If some adhesive still clings, use benzine. If this does not remove all adhesive, put on rubber gloves and clean the mosaic with a 10% solution of hydrochloric acid.

DIRECT METHOD USING MAGNESITE

Rough materials such as crystals, irregular stones, or materials of different thicknesses are most safely embedded in mortar if magnesite is used as a binding material. In contrast to adhesive, magnesite provides a versatile setting bed in which tesserae can be tipped or angled at will. Magnesite is also the best material to use when working with rough tesserae which cannot be grouted (Figure 18). Color is mixed directly into the mortar.

FIGURE 18. Use of rough material which cannot be grouted.

To construct a mosaic using magnesite mix, design a cartoon and prepare a base board, as in Chapter 3. Then, guided by the cartoon, choose mosaic material (Figure 19). Lay this material directly on the

FIGURE 19. Choosing material for mosaic.

cartoon or, if a cartoon is large, divide it into sections. When choosing material, keep in mind not only color areas but texture. This step of the work will take considerable attention if materials other than traditional mosaic glass are incorporated. Remember, variety in the size of tesserae arouses interest. Generally speaking, large areas of background will require larger tesserae than the smaller more involved parts of a design. In selecting material, move the tesserae about, exchange them, try one against another, brilliant against dull. This can become a very fascinating game and should always be played before tesserae are set into the magnesite. After tesserae have been set and the mortar hardened, mistakes are impossible to correct except through considerable effort with a hammer and chisel.

When all material has been chosen, glue a sample of each kind of tessera to its corresponding area on the cartoon. In this way, no sample will be forgotten if work is prolonged. While setting tesserae into mortar, pin the cartoon on a wall where it can be used for reference.

Mosaic is laid in sections according to color areas. When ready

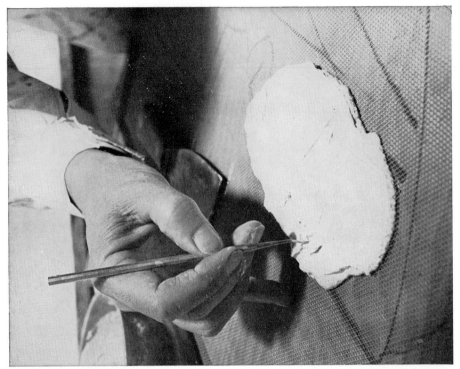

FIGURE 21. Marking design in wet magnesite.

FIGURE 20. Spreading magnesite.

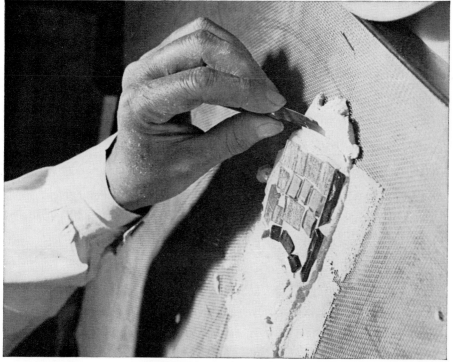

FIGURE 23. Cutting away excess magnesite.

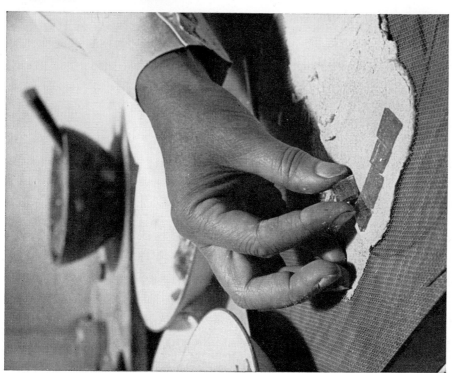

FIGURE 22. Placing tesserae.

to set tesserae, mix a batch of magnesite according to Chapter 6. The amount of mortar mixed is guided by color areas, for color must be mixed directly into the magnesite when grouting is impossible or undesirable. If a very small area of magnesite requires color, sprinkle dry coloring powder directly on the magnesite after it has been spread on the board. Press the color in with a spatula. This technique saves mixing a dab of magnesite.

Mix only a small amount of magnesite to start, as one works slowly at first and excess magnesite is often wasted through hardening. Remember to use outdoor waterproof magnesite if a garden piece is planned.

With a spatula, spread the magnesite mix about ¼ inch thick, working it well into the screening on the base board (Figure 20). The thickness of a setting bed is determined by tessera size. Larger stones require a thicker layer of mortar. Where different sizes of tesserae are used, spread the magnesite thickly enough to imbed the larger pieces and yet keep a uniform thickness of mortar throughout.

When magnesite is spread on a base board, it covers the guide lines of a design. However, the artist can retain these lines if he spreads the magnesite in small areas at one time. Refer to the finished cartoon often. With a sharp tool (a dentist's probe is good) redraw the guide lines in the wet magnesite (Figure 21).

Now begin laying tesserae. These are placed in rows and pressed firmly into the magnesite (Figure 22). Remember to follow the contours of a design. Tesserae must be pressed securely into the magnesite to provide adequate binding, but the magnesite should not rise to the top of the stones. Generally, tesserae should protrude slightly above the level of the setting bed. If a tessera is pressed too firmly and becomes submerged in magnesite, remove it with a tweezer and wash before re-using.

When setting a large plain area of mosaic in a uniform color, vary the tesserae somewhat. This practice eliminates monotony. For example, in a red background use a few pieces of green or tan. In gold backgrounds include a few plain yellow or tan stones.

After one section of a mosaic has been completed, cut away excess magnesite from its outer edges (Figure 23). This is done to preserve a clean outline or section of color. A fresh batch of magnesite can then be mixed and another section of mosaic laid.

If there is a time lapse between work on adjoining sections, finished work should be thoroughly wet before fresh magnesite is placed on the board. If this is not done, the dry section, acting like a sponge, will absorb liquid from the newly placed magnesite. Then the magnesite will neither bind properly to the board nor hold the tesserae. Days and weeks may be required to construct a mosaic, so always be sure that the previous day's work is thoroughly wet down with water. When magnesite is used, it is well *not* to lay a damp cloth over the work. This may provoke a harmful chemical reaction. A bloom or a white film may form on the surface of the mortar when it is dry, destroying its color.

FIGURE 24. Cleaning mosaic.

When the finished mosaic is thoroughly dry, clean it by removing any specks of mortar on the surface with a small tool such as a dentist's chisel (Figure 24). Then rub clean with a cloth dampened with water. If the mosaic is composed of glass, it can be cleaned easily with a cloth and a window cleaner.

8

Supplementary Practice in the Direct Method

The artist who uses varied mosaic materials in a base of magnesite has advanced into a medium both complex and full of rewards. The following supplementary practices are suggested for those whose experience with magnesite has been slight. They will prove valuable to the inexperienced, to the person who wishes to experiment, and to those wishing to perfect a specific technique.

No material need be wasted in these practices. Scrape up the tesserae while the magnesite is still soft. Tesserae may be thrown in a sieve, washed with running water, and used again.

Texture

Texture is often as important as color in a work of mosaic art. For instance, the same blue may be had in glass or in a mineral. However, the *effect* produced by an area of blue glass is vastly different from that of an area of a blue mineral, such as chrysocolla. One can learn this difference in texture-effect only by working with the mosaic materials themselves. A preliminary drawing or cartoon on paper can never indicate texture effects. This is so true that, when submitting a sketch or cartoon to a client, a mosaicist always includes samples of mosaic materials to be used (Figure 25).

Make: a small sample of board and magnesite. Divide this square into several sections. Selecting one color but different materials, fill these sections. For example, choose the color brown. Try stained glass, ceramic tile, encaustic tile, lave, Italian Smalti, Venetian glass, etc. Notice that cutting material into different sizes also changes its texture (Figure 25-A).

46

FIGURE 25. Differences in texture.

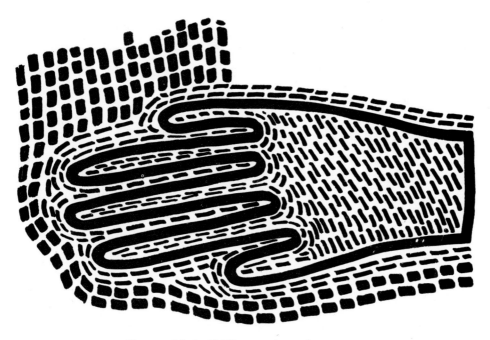

FIGURE 25-A. Different sizes of tesserae.

Reflected Light

Mosaic becomes radiant when light is reflected from the surface of its tesserae. It differs in this respect from stained glass, which gains brilliance when penetrated by light. When a mosaic is horizontal on a work table instead of vertical on a wall, its reflected light value is changed. For this reason, mosaics executed on a horizontal surface should occasionally be placed upright for viewing. An artist can control light reflection to some extent by tipping the tesserae at different angles. This variation adds interest to the mosaic.

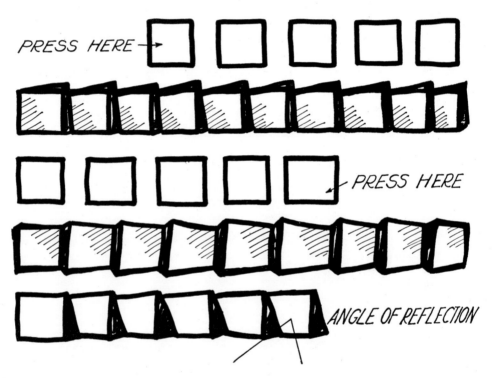

FIGURE 26. Tipping of tesserae for reflected light.

Make: a small sample of board and magnesite. Lightly lay tesserae flat on the magnesite. Then take a stick or dental tool (fingers are too blunt) and press the edges of the individual tesserae into different angles. When this has been done, notice how the sample looks on a table or propped up against a wall. At night, move a lamp from one side of the mosaic to another and study the effect (Figure 26).

Distance to Be Viewed

Distance and the angle from which a mosaic is viewed must also be considered. Overcomplicated designs become lost when viewed from a distance. The angle of vision can also distort a design. Because distance and the angle of vision affect a mosaic, it is important to view unfinished work from a distance. If a piece of work is not too large to move conveniently, set it against a wall. Stand far back and study it occasionally, much as a sculptor studies a statue. If a piece of work is too heavy to move, climb on a ladder and study it through a diminishing glass. An inspection like this may save disappointment later. Areas in which values are blurred or lost can be corrected before the mosaic hardens.

Make: trial squares, stressing strong and subtle contrasts. Vary thickness of line and color. View these pieces from a distance of sixty

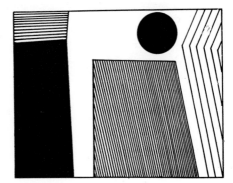

FIGURE 27. Distance observation.

feet. Study them to see which parts are retained at this distance and which are lost. If a studio is not large enough for this long view, set the pieces outdoors (Figure 27).

Contours

Mosaic tesserae are generally laid to follow the outlines of a form. Highlight and depth are developed through contours. This process also gives the work a rhythm that is all-important. Rhythm which comes from following contours is especially necessary in modern abstract designs where texture, harmony, and color complete the composition in which no form or object is discernible. When working with figures, make sure the tesserae follow the flow of drapery and form of body muscles. In laying a face, it is best to start with the eyes and nose and follow these contours, since they are the most prominent (Figure 28).

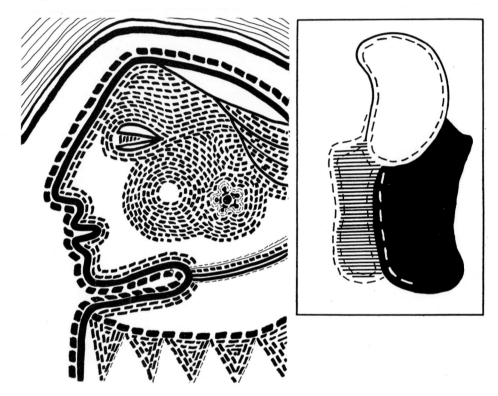

FIGURES 28 AND 29. Contours.

Make: a small sample of board and magnesite. Mix three mortars of different colors. Slap them down freely on the board and spread them out, letting the mortars meet in a haphazard way. Then lay tesserae by following the lines where these mortars meet. Work from the outlines of each color, matching the tesserae to mortar color. This practice is an excellent one for learning to work spontaneously, as well as for following contours (Figure 29).

Material

Mosaic material must be handled with respect. It has its own way of wanting to go. Like a sculptor who in carving must respect the grain of his wood, so the mosaicist must respect the relations of different textures, the affinities of stone and glass. To the mosaicist, every permanent and colorful material soon becomes a potential source of supply. Self-restraint is necessary. Materials from the same source form a unified whole, such as using all glass or all stone. Also, when one kind of material is used exclusively, it will not present so many pitfalls for the beginner. Mixing materials is more difficult. Then, too, the temptation to use novel materials such as jewels and bits of enamel, brass, or iron can cheapen work. It is only after much experience in making mosaics that these novelties can be introduced with taste and discretion.

Although there is no rule as to which combinations of materials will work well and which badly, it is generally true that brighter stones, ones that catch and reflect light, should be used in smaller areas. In choosing materials, one should estimate in advance how much to prepare for each area in the mosaic. All material should be cut before work is begun. This prevents interrupting the work in order to cut more tesserae. Nothing is more frustrating than to find a shortage of prepared material when the magnesite is hardening.

9

The Reverse Method

The reverse or indirect method is one in which tesserae are pasted on paper, then the whole turned upside down and pressed into wet mortar. There are two important advantages to this method. First, a more level surface may be obtained when tesserae are reversed en masse than when they are set into the mortar individually. Tables, floors, murals, and large architectural pieces requiring a smooth surface are usually constructed by the reverse method. Second, a mosaic made according to the reverse method may be easily corrected. Tesserae are laid directly on the outlines of a cartoon before being pressed into mortar. At this stage, it is possible to see the relationship of each piece of tessera to the whole mosaic. Material can then be exchanged, colors shifted, outlines strengthened, mistakes corrected, before the tesserae are set in mortar.

Many artists find the reverse method of working quite compatible. They like the freedom to make revisions and to remove or change pieces, a freedom seldom possible when tesserae are set directly into mortar. In the direct method, tesserae *can* be removed while the mortar is wet, but sometimes an artist does not notice a mistake for several days. Correcting in the direct method then becomes a laborious process of chiseling away hard concrete. In the reverse method, however, correcting is done during the design stage.

There is no hard-and-fast rule as to whether mosaics should be laid in the direct or the reverse method. There is a traditional way which has endured for centuries in Italy: pasting tesserae on paper when making large mosaics; setting tesserae directly into mortar when constructing smaller ones. But even this rule is violated, as the Italians sometimes use the reverse method to make small portable mosaics. So let us repeat: there is no hard-and-fast rule; there are two basic methods with continual variations. The mosaicist working and experimenting on his own is apt to discover a method or variation of a method that pleases him. What he does today will probably be different from what he does five years from now. Consequently, this chapter will present the traditional approach to the reverse method, demonstrated with photographs of the working process of Joseph Young, a prominent mosaicist of Los Angeles, California. This will serve as a guide in this technique, regardless of whether the mosaic is a large wall mural or a small portable.

The designing, enlarging, and cartoon are drawn in the same way as in the direct method, as outlined previously. After the cartoon has been finished, it is cut into sections and numbered according to corresponding sections in the original cartoon (Figure 30).

FIGURE 30. Division of cartoon.

A simple paste of flour and water is made to fasten tesserae to the cartoon. The quality of this paste assumes considerable importance. It must be sufficiently strong to hold the tesserae in place even during shipping, and yet permit the paper to be removed easily when the mosaic is installed.

FIGURE 31. Pasting tesserae to cartoon.

FIGURE 32. Stacking of pasted sections of cartoon

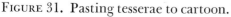

There is a fundamental recipe for making flour and water paste. Combine one part flour with eight parts water. Boil this mixture for five minutes, strain out any lumps, and use. This paste will keep tesserae in place, yet will allow the paper to be easily removed when the tesserae have been reversed into mortar. Do not attempt to use a glue or strong paste when laying tesserae in the reverse method. Such adhesives will make the paper difficult to remove. Steam cleaning a mosaic is a complicated, expensive and time-consuming process. It is also an unnecessary one. Mosaicists often experiment to find the "perfect" proportions of flour and water. If a mosaicist achieves a paste above average, he will usually keep its recipe a trade secret. However, craftsmen in the tile trade have done considerable experimenting with paste and even have a sum of money set aside in their Union for educational work concerning mosaic. The advice of these men, essential when installing large mosaics, is also helpful when it comes to the proportions of a flour and water paste.

When pasting, brush each tessera with paste and set it against the cartoon, following the contours of the design (Figure 31). Keep the tesserae close together, but allow at least one sixteenth of an inch between them. This space is necessary for grouting. The sections of pasted tesserae may then be stacked in sequence and transported to their destination (Figure 32).

A mosaic mural is generally installed by competent and experienced workmen, tile setters who have a knowledge of mosaic. At this point

FIGURE 33. Grouting of section.

FIGURE 34. Applying section to prepared wall.

FIGURE 35. Removal of paper.

theories cannot take the place of experience. The amount of moisture in a setting bed must be carefully judged. If a mural is on a vertical surface and the mortar is too wet, the whole mosaic may begin to slide downwards. There is also the question of how much mosaic can be installed before the setting bed hardens. Problems like these require the assistance of an expert tile man. Such craftsmen are not easily located in the United States, where mosaic is in its infancy, but most major tile houses can recommend one or two of them.

When the mosaic is finally ready to be installed, an area of wall is spread with a setting layer of mortar. This mortar should have a stiff consistency, similar to butter at room temperature. If a mortar is too soft and watery, it will loosen the tesserae from their paper and cause them to sink too deeply into the setting bed. The area of wall spread with mortar is determined by the amount of mosaic that can be set before the mortar hardens. In the United States, mosaic is generally laid from the bottom of a structure upwards. This method is directly opposite to that followed in Europe.

After the wall has been prepared, the sections of pasted tesserae are laid paper side down on a table and a setting layer of cement troweled into the cracks between the stones (Figure 33). Then the section of tesserae is placed on the wall, paper side out. Gradually the tesserae are worked into the mortar. They are tapped gently with a hammer, or a board is used to press them down until they are evenly embedded in the mortar (Figure 34).

When a section of wall has been completed and the mortar hardened sufficiently so that the tesserae will not be dislodged (usually in a few hours), it is time to strip off the paper. The timing here is delicate. If a mortar is allowed to set completely, mistakes will be arduous to correct. On the other hand, if a mortar is too wet, the position of the tesserae will be disturbed and the design perhaps ruined when the paper is removed. The paper should be made thoroughly wet before it is removed (Figure 35).

After the mosaic is completely set, it is given a final scrubbing and any stubborn spots of excess cement removed with a solution of muriatic acid (Figure 36).

A finished mural is shown here (Figure 37).

The same procedure is followed if a small portable mosaic is done according to the reverse method. When a mosaic is no larger than a foot square it is not necessary to cut the cartoon in sections. Such port-

FIGURE 36. Cleaning of installed mosaic.

FIGURE 37. Mosaic mural for Los Angeles Police Facilities
Building.

able mosaics may have an ordinary plywood or composition board base, as used in the direct method. The base is covered with a layer of setting cement. The paper of tesserae is then reversed onto the mortar and the tesserae pressed down gently just as on a wall.

Tables, counters and other pieces of furniture decorated with mosaic laid in the reverse method frequently require a frame. Mosaic kits for decorating furniture usually include this frame. The mosaicist who does not use a kit must have frames made at a metal works. This need not be too expensive. A frame for a mosaic table, for instance, is simply constructed, having legs and an edged top into which the base containing the mosaic is set.

10

Italian Methods

Present-day Italy produces few mosaics of contemporary design. However, when it comes to art following traditional designs, Italy remains the mosaic center of the world. This is because few artists have equaled the Italians in technical skill and in copying processes. From Italy mosaics are shipped throughout the world, to be installed in churches and large-scale public buildings. The mosaics themselves are made in privately owned studios. The largest of these studios is the Vatican workshop, a vast mosaic factory the standards of which are perfection and fidelity to detail.

Italians approach mosaic-making with an attitude which has been developed over generations. The techniques of mosaic art, like an ancient craft, are passed from father to son. When a mosaic is made in Italy, work progresses slowly. Time does not count as it does in the United States. Traditional methods of mosaic art are employed and indeed preferred to any "short cut" process. For example, each tiny tessera used by the Italians in making floor and table mosaics has a slight bevel, so that the stones will set firmly but will not show any mortar. To cut this bevel requires hours and days of time. Most American artists would grow exasperated! Not so the Italians.

Italian mosaic studios customarily hire from four to twelve or more workers as their business fluctuates. Tools, materials, and methods of the various studios in Rome are similar. Hence a description of one studio only, that of Guilo Giovannetti, is given.

The Guilo Giovannetti studio operates with one head designer, two or three very skilled craftsmen, and a few other workers who are apprentices. Occasionally there are some women workers in the studio, but this is a recent innovation. When mosaic is laid according to a design, only skilled craftsmen are allowed to work on hands and faces.

Less skilled craftsmen are given draperies and floral pieces, while young apprentices work all day on backgrounds. Every part of the work is directed by the head designer. This man also chooses and mixes tesserae. Background colors for a mosaic are mixed in proper proportions and then set aside in bins for the workers. From a distance most backgrounds look like solid color, but they are actually a blend of colors carefully proportioned by the head designer.

FIGURE 38. Wall mosaic from Nea Moni Monastery, Island of Chios, Greece.

When a mosaic is done by the reverse method, a cartoon is made and divided into sections. These sections are in turn divided among the workers. After tesserae have been laid, the sections are reassembled and formed into a whole mosaic. At all times a large color cartoon of the project hangs upon a wall where the workers may refer to it.

Fixed-in-Place

Cement is the mortar used when mosaics are set in place on large outdoor walls and floors. A rough bed of concrete is poured, and over this a setting bed is laid in sections sufficient to cover the work that one man can achieve before the concrete hardens, which is in approximately three hours. This setting bed of concrete is mixed by volume in the following proportions:

> 8/10 cement (in America we would use Portland cement)
> 1/10 aged lime putty
> 1/10 marble dust

Water is added to form a paste the consistency of glazier's putty or potter's clay.

Portable

Italian portable mosaics are executed in a very different procedure. Work is generally done by the direct method. A base for the mosaic rests on a slanted table or easel and the mosaic itself is constructed by one craftsman. Tesserae are set into the mortar with infinite care. Rulers are used to maintain precise lines. Sometimes the tesserae used in this work are so small that they become like jewelry and must be set with a magnifying glass. These portable pieces of mosaic are technically magnificent. Esthetically, the work often has a too-finished, static appearance. Little or no experimental work is encouraged. Many of these mosaics have subtle shadings and resemble paintings. They are no longer mosaics in terms of simple direct forms.

The base for portable mosaics is usually steel. It is a panel composed of sheet iron which has a quarter-inch binding of brass screwed around its edges. Steel provides a permanent frame and bed for mosaic, but it is extremely heavy. To form a bind with the mortar, the sheet metal is roughed into points with a chisel. In very large mosaics where a more rigid backing is needed, a layer of cement reinforced by steel rods is poured on the steel. On this layer, the mosaic is laid in a setting bed.

Once the steel base has been constructed, a tracing of the cartoon is made and is fastened to the base with dabs of mortar. Then small sections of the tracing are snipped out and replaced by tesserae. Generally speaking, a design is cut out along its contours. As only a small part of the tracing is removed at one time, it is easy for a worker to follow a design. In this manner, Italian mosaics are built up slowly. When a mosaic has been completed, excess mortar is scraped away from the tesserae and they are cleaned with gasoline.

The setting bed for portable mosaics is made of "stucco." Italians use the word "stucco" when they wish to convey the meaning of the English word "mortar." Stucco, as used in Italy, varies little from its ancient counterpart. It is a laborious material to mix. However, once mixed, stucco can be used for three or four days before it hardens. This is a great advantage over quicker-setting mortars. Also, stucco can be

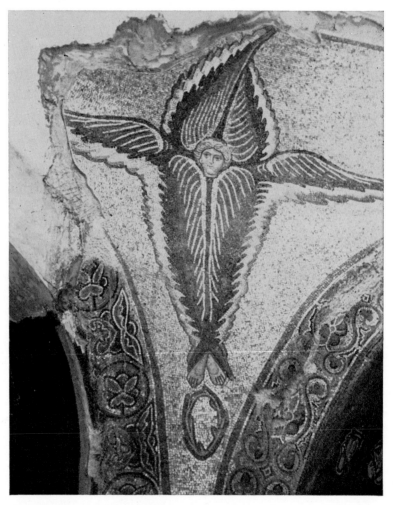

FIGURE 39. Archangel from wall mosaic, Nea Moni Monastery, Island of Chios, Greece.

ground to a very fine finish suitable for tables and floors. The formula for Italian stucco is:

1 part brick dust (this means grinding bricks to a very fine powder)
1 part marble dust
1 part lime putty aged at least two months
3 parts boiled linseed oil

Mix ingredients to a dough-like consistency. On a slab, flatten dough until it is approximately 1″ thick. Cut the mixture into squares 4″ x 6″ before it dries. When dry these squares may be stacked and stored for future use. Drying time will vary according to climate, from two weeks in summer to two months in winter.

When ready to make stucco, pulverize as many squares as needed for three or four days work. Roll these squares into a fine dust, using a bottle or rolling pin. Place some dust on a marble slab. Add a few drops of liquid: 1 part raw to 4 parts boiled linseed oil. With a flat trowel mix this oil well into the dust. Add only a little oil and work the mixture continuously and patiently. Then slowly add remaining marble dust and mix until the stucco has a consistency like plasticine or butter at room temperature.

The Vatican Studio

Mosaic-making methods in the Vatican studio and workshop do not vary much from the private mosaic studios in Italy. The Vatican studio is, however, famous for the volume of work it produces. An enormous amount of material is kept on hand. This material is stored in a supply room which resembles the safety deposit vault of a modern bank. It is a vast room with long corridors stretching into the distance. These corridors are lined with steel filing cabinets containing numbered drawers. Above them is another floor with a second layer of filing cabinets, all containing Smalti in every conceivable shade. The glass is manufactured at Murano, and every color is produced and numbered so that the most realistic oil paintings can be copied. Some stored Smalti still carries the Vatican stamp, although mosaic glass has not been manufactured at the Vatican for more than twenty years.

In the mosaic studio itself sit many workers, each before a tilted table or easel holding a piece of work. Near each craftsman is a table containing tesserae, tools, stucco, and a block of wood in which a hardie is embedded for cutting material. Above the craftsman is the photograph or picture he is transforming into mosaic. Two sides of the Vatican workroom are filled by cases containing numbered samples of each shade of Smalti. The workers can choose an exact shade of glass and obtain it from the supply room.

Cartoons are drawn on a studio wall over one hundred feet long. This wall is slanted slightly from the floor. Close to the wall are large plywood forms duplicating the sizes of domes and curved walls of churches. Using these forms, a mosaic may be constructed to fit church architecture exactly.

Frequently mosaics made at the Vatican studio are set in temporary stucco. This material contains so much oil that it never hardens completely. Afer a mosaic is assembled and laid into the stucco, a material somewhat stiffer than cheese cloth is pasted on the surface of the tesserae. Then the mosaic is reversed and the temporary stucco cleaned away. Tweezers and probes like dentist's tools are used to remove excess stucco. Mosaics finished in this fashion are stacked and stored to await installation.

Mosaic Filato

Filato, or "thread," is a word which describes a type of tesserae used to make minute Italian mosaics. Brightly decorative and hand-set, this mosaic has always been popular in Italy but is little known in the United States. Frequently filato is seen in jewelry. These small pieces of jewelry, sometimes less than one inch square, have intricately inlaid tesserae which give them a special appeal. The tesserae in these mosaics are made from long thread-like rods, which are cut and the pieces fitted into the mosaic with tweezers. The mosaics themselves are usually constructed under a magnifying glass.

Mosaic filato is made by an interesting process which may be duplicated in any home or studio. Smalti is melted and reformed into long rods which can then be notched with a file and snapped off. This process is also used in making vari-colored filato. Different quantities of colored Smalti are melted and fused while still hot. Filato may be made by the following steps:

Tools: small blowtorch
2 awls approximately 10″ long
Crucible 18″ long with a triangular piece on the bottom to keep it from tipping.
Marble or granite slabs 3″ deep and 12″ square.
Steel form as in Figure 40-D.

1. Cut Smalti in pieces ¼″ square and place them in the crucible. The crucible should be set on a marble slab to prevent burning of tables or other furniture. The points of the two awls are also put in the crucible (Figure 40-A and B).

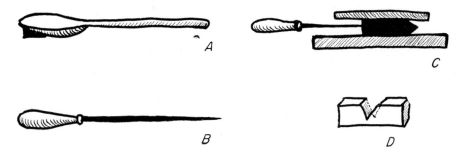

FIGURE 40. Tools used in making Italian filato.

2. Hold blowtorch at a tilted angle and heat Smalti. When the glass begins to soften, work the point of one awl into the hot mass. Twisting, work the point of the second awl into the glass.

3. Set the blowtorch upright and let it stand alone. Lift the mass of hot Smalti up to the flame. Rotate awls and mass of liquefied Smalti until it is thoroughly mixed. This will take five to ten minutes.

4. Work mass of Smalti off one awl by twisting the awl point loose.

5. Holding Smalti with the other awl, take the mass to a granite slab. Using another small block of granite, shape the mass into square sides. Rub it to bevel one end and to form a four-sided point (Figure 40-C).

6. Reheat Smalti in the blowtorch. With tweezers, grab a bit of the point of the hot Smalti and draw it out 8″ or 10″. Snap off the end with a twist of the wrist.

7. Keeping the Smalti hot, draw out the four-sided filato. Turn both the awl and the Smalti's end, now held in fingers or gloves, to keep glass hot on all four sides. Vary the thickness of the filato rod to get all sizes for future use.

8. When a long piece of filato is drawn out, set it on the table. Snap the rod off and repeat the process until all the hot Smalti is used. Allow the rods to cool for approximately ten minutes. They may then be filed and broken at will.

9. When square or triangular rods are desired, press them while still hot into a steel form such as shown in Figure 40-D.

11

Pebble Mosaic

The pebble is a humble object. It is beautiful because it has been a victim: wind-worn, wave-washed, crushed, rolled, the pebble remains subject to and takes the form of nature. Ever since man has seen and felt pebbles, he has invented things to do with them. Mosaic was one of his earliest inventions. As man walked on pebbles, he began to place them in permanent patterns. Soon floors, streets, and courtyards were royally decorated.

Today pebbles are still used to decorate the courtyard, a region usually known to Americans as the patio. In small areas, pebbles may be embedded in home-made concrete blocks. When large areas are being covered, the pebbles are often laid in a wet concrete slab. Pebbles have also found their way into wall panels and into the advanced fine art of mosaic as seen in art galleries, churches, and public buildings. Working with pebbles has become quite a sophisticated occupation!

Pebble patios not only add interest and graciousness to any garden, they are a good exercise for the beginner in mosaic. A simple method of constructing a pebble patio is to make a series of circular concrete blocks. These blocks are then treated much like brick. They can be laid in a loose bed of dampened sand or set in concrete. They can be used as stepping stones, stairs, or placed one on top of another to decorate a wall. The outdoor pebble emblem illustrated in Figure 45 may be made by the following steps:

1. On a piece of greased plywood or paper, draw a circle 16″ in diameter. An easy way of forming this circle is to stick an icepick firmly in the plywood's center. Loop a string around the pick. At the desired radius, tie the opposite end of the string around a pencil and inscribe a circle. This method of drawing a circle can be used no matter what size circle is needed. A circle in the garden may be drawn by driving a stake into the ground, using a cord and sharp stick to inscribe the form.

2. Bend a piece of brass or plastic binding 3/4″ wide around the circle. Let the edges of this binding overlap; they do not have to meet precisely, as their purpose is to hold mortar in place. Hammer nails around the outside of this binding to keep it in shape (Figure 42).

3. Roughly sketch a design on the plywood. This design should be extremely simple. Small pebble mosaics are pleasing only when their lines are fundamental. Rows of dark and light pebbles are often laid freehand, with a result that gives these mosaics a special charm. However, when more intricate designs, such as initials, are used, they should first be designed on paper.

4. Place a piece of wire mesh or expanded metal inside the circle. The mesh need not be cut to a circular form but should fill the greater part of the circle. This material provides reinforcing, so the concrete will not crack when handled. When reinforcing is used, concrete thickness may be reduced by approximately half.

5. Mix a bowl of outdoor or waterproof magnesite (Sculptor Mix). Approximately five quarts of magnesite will be required for a circle 16″ in diameter. The waterproofing chemical in the magnesite will cause it to dry a blue-green shade. If this color is not desired, mix coloring in the dry magnesite before adding the chloride solution. Work

FIGURE 41. Mosaic from Chinese patio.

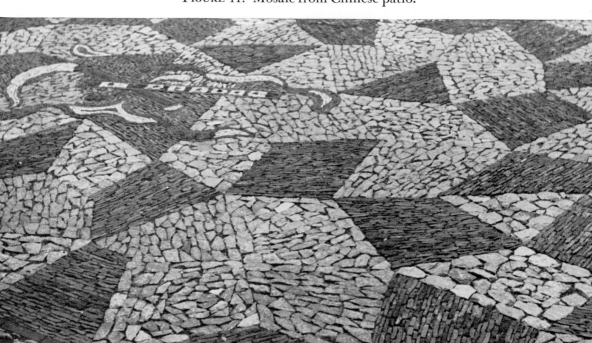

FIGURE 42. Base and binding of pebble emblem.

FIGURE 43. Spreading of magnesite.

FIGURE 44. Placing tesserae.

FIGURE 45. Finished pebble emblem used in patio.

the magnesite until it has a consistency like firm biscuit dough. Place the mix in the center of the plywood and spread it evenly outwards. Repeat this process until the magnesite is level with the binding (Figure 43).

6. After leveling the mortar with a trowel or stick, mark both its center and the divisions of the design to be formed. Beginning at the mosaic's center, lay pebbles or other tesserae outwards. Make the most of contrasting colors, shapes, angles, or textures, laying areas of first one kind and then another (Figure 44). (Finished mosaic: Figure 45.)

Smaller outdoor plaques may be made by using aluminum pie tins. Grease the tins to prevent the magnesite from sticking. These plaques are ideal projects for children either at school or at home, because they can be made anywhere, even on a kitchen table spread with newspapers. If children are working, ready-mix mortar will prove more convenient than magnesite. The aluminum pie tins may be used over and over again.

A similar method of laying a pebble patio is to make a series of square or rectangular concrete blocks. These blocks are best made in sizes approximating 2' x 2' x 2" deep. Bigger blocks will be cumbersome to move. To make one concrete block: First construct a square form of 2" x 4" boards. Do not nail three corners of this form but fasten them together with hinges. Fasten the fourth corner of the form with a hasp such as is used on a gate, or a common hook and eye. When the form has been constructed, lay it on a piece of heavy paper or greased plywood.

Then mix a setting base of concrete, one part cement to three parts sand. Coloring powder, if desired, should be blended with dry cement. Add water until the mix is the consistency of a thick cake batter. To every gallon of water, stir in two or three tablespoons of plastic cement glue. This glue will increase the adhesive power of the concrete to hold smooth-surfaced pebbles. Pour the concrete mixture into the form. Then lay pebbles in place on the concrete surface. After several hours, the block will be sufficiently dry for the form to be removed and used to make another block. To remove the form, simply unfasten its hasp and swing its hinged sides apart from the cast block.

Finished concrete work should always be allowed to set slowly. Keep the blocks moist by sprinkling or by covering them with damp cloths. To clean excess concrete from pebble mosaic, use a stiff wire brush and muriatic acid. Wear a pair of rubber gloves to protect the hands. The blocks are then ready to be set loosely in the garden or laid in a concrete slab or wall.

Both the circle and the square block methods of making a pebble patio have several advantages. Time and materials are under control. A person limited in time can accomplish a small amount of work at one session. Naturally, more than one form can be used if a person desires to make blocks rapidly. The work itself is not tiring, as a project involving concrete is often apt to be. Lastly, the block method of laying a patio is not absolutely dependent on the setting time of the mortar involved. Concrete in large areas is a tricky substance, and an inexperienced craftsman sometimes finds the mortar hardening before all the tesserae can be laid.

Laying pebbles is not a tedious job, but their effect can be tedious unless a few rules are observed. A pebble design gains its form from areas of stones which have unified color, shape, and size. Group the pebbles according to these qualities, and a design will have both shape and contrast. Texture also plays a major part in pebble mosaic. Capitalize on the shapes of stones. Sometimes it is best to set a group of flat stones edgewise; sometimes they are best when left flat or tipped at an angle. The artist will improvise and learn as he works. However, press all stones into the concrete firmly. If they are not embedded deeply enough, they will be loosened from the mortar as people walk over them.

FIGURE 46. Fireplace in pebble and marble mosaic, by Louisa Jenkins.

12

Children's Mosaics and Classes in Mosaic

Whenever children are exposed to mosaics, it is a case of love at first sight. Children are artists from birth. Their senses, like new leaves, have not yet shriveled, nor do they take objects for granted. They have not, as adults have, been long divorced from the pleasure of discovering objects through their textural qualities. Texture—that quality in mosaic responsible for so much beauty but rarely noticed—is immediately appreciated by children. Except for those in certain professions such as sculpture or weaving, adults have forgotten to observe texture. In observing things grown people use their eyes almost exclusively and must turn to the blind, who "see" the world through their fingers, to discover how completely objects can be enjoyed and understood by touch. Children do not need to learn from the blind. They are close to the beginnings of knowledge. A child discovering the world about him gets down to fundamentals: he picks up, tastes, tears apart, strokes and smashes objects. Is it any wonder that the texture of mosaic appeals to children more strongly than the arts of drawing or painting!

Teaching children mosaic can be an inspiring process. Naturally, how mosaic is taught will depend on the ages of the children involved. With small children, it is best to present a well-limited supply of tesserae, keeping this material separated in shoe boxes. Encourage an older child to make a drawing of his project. This design should be extremely simple. Young children will enjoy designing spontaneously as they set the tesserae. Suggest that children use basic forms such as lines, squares and circles. However, after suggesting that a design be kept simple, it is best for an adult to step aside. Let a teacher or parent possess the humility to give children their due. Children have their own ways of seeing and usually an imagination far more vivid than their teachers. A wise teacher or parent will not attempt to superimpose the adult's more stultified view on a child, will not influence a child's expression or curb its spontaneity. On the contrary, an adult artist may learn from watching a child.

Safety precautions when working with children are few but essential. Children from kindergarten through the fourth grade should never be given glass with sharp edges or material which might cause a cut. Blunt-edged pebbles, tile, shells and marbles make excellent materials for young children. Such materials are easiest to handle when in fairly large pieces. Children over the age of ten may be given glass and other materials with sharp edges, provided they are instructed how to handle them. However, no group of children should ever be permitted to use glass unless the group is small enough for individual supervision. Above all, the teacher must emphasize care in handling glass and the avoidance of sharp edges. A demonstration should be made of how to pick up glass by grasping its flat surfaces.

Some materials used in setting mosaic are harmful to the eyes and these should not be used when working with children. Rubber base mastics and certain glues fall into this category. These materials are sticky and may be inadvertently transferred from fingers to eyes when children rub their faces. For this reason spackle is the best setting material to use in a group of young children. Spackle is a non-irritating plasterer's compound which can be purchased at hardware or paint stores.

To avoid confusion, cut materials for children in advance. However, when a group is small, children like to cut their own tesserae and should not be denied the fun of this experience. Young people can quickly learn to use tile nippers. Of course, children should never be allowed to cut or shatter glass.

Since children spend most of their young lives at home, the home is a natural place to teach mosaic. What better cooperation can there be than that in which a family creates together? Father, mother, and children of all ages can make a mosaic. Each child assumes responsibility for, and executes a part of, the mosaic. The sense of group workmanship, of constructive harmony which stems from such projects, is perhaps the best antidote to a violent and often destructive age. The child learns creative cooperation while he is very impressionable and in the group he loves best—his family. Furthermore, nothing delights a child more than to examine a finished mosaic and see with pride his own part in the work.

A mosaic made by Dr. and Mrs. Carl Werts and their five children demonstrates the success of family art. The Werts were rewarded not only by having a mosaic which has won state-wide acclaim, but by the creative experience they shared with their children, an experience so rare because of the age barriers between members of a family. Dr. and Mrs. Werts live in Los Angeles, and their children are four, six, nine,

FIGURE 47. Werts children making mosaic.

FIGURE 48. Finished mosaic by family of Dr. Francis Werts, Los Angeles.

eleven, and twelve years of age. It was decided to let the children design the mosaic, and so a large plywood base was ruled off into sections and each child made responsible for a section. Work was done in the family's breakfast room. Saturdays and Sundays were devoted to mosaic-making. Watching television was voluntarily curtailed, and within a month the mosaic was completed. It is a colorful, imaginative and strong expression of a family's faith in God (Figure 48).

The decision to let the children design this mosaic seemed an impractical one at first. When the children began work they each made a human head so large that it looked as if the rest of their design would not fit in. However, the children defended their right to design against the suggestions of older people, and they were correct! The mosaic, when finished, has an abstract and arresting composition which compares with and challenges the work of more literal adult artists.

It is but one jump from family to school. Mosaics, having proved their value in the home, are appearing more and more frequently in the classroom. That they can form a vital though inexpensive part of American education was shown by the Anna Conlon Memorial mosaic made at Hillcrest School in San Francisco. Anna Conlon was principal of Hillcrest for many years, and when she died those who loved her decided to erect a memorial. Mosaic was chosen because it was hoped that in that case all the school children could participate. Emmy Lou Packard, a San Francisco artist, was invited to design and direct the project. Parents, principal, teachers and the director of Art Education for San Francisco city schools cooperated with Miss Packard. The children gathered much of their own material. School buses took them to beaches where they collected pebbles. These trips led in turn to essays and compositions on mosaics, and so their project was incorporated into other parts of the school curriculum. Soon a vast amount of materials—glass, shells, pebbles, and all sorts of objects, including butterfly collections brought from home—had been gathered. Very little material was purchased.

Work on the mosaic commenced after a design by Miss Packard had been enlarged and traced on plywood panels. The children, 650 of them from kindergarten through the sixth grade, came to the studio-room in small groups. They worked for fifteen-minute periods, each child setting a few stones. Miss Packard executed the more complicated parts of the mosaic herself, but left all other sections and even much of the design to the children. Daily, then, the basic principles of art were demonstrated—not preached—for and by the children. Says Miss Packard of the children: "I treated them like adults and they behaved better than adults."

After twenty-seven days the memorial was completed—a mosaic 6' x 21'. Truly in speed this work rivals that of the old Byzantine church mosaicists. Its 50,000 tessarae are glued to plywood with tile-setter's mastic. This mastic shows through the children's work and yet when seen from a normal viewing distance enriches it. The mosaic is a remarkable one. Naturally the children feel it is theirs. One small boy summed up the attitude of his schoolmates. Studying the finished mural, he said, "It's the loveliest mosaic I have ever seen. It's better than anyone in our class could do. Or anyone in the world." He pointed. "It has the Negro people. It has the fishermen. It has the Chinese people. It has the birds and butterflies." Then he added thoughtfully, "Miss Conlon must have been a wonderful person." (Figure 49.)

FIGURE 49. Construction of Anna Conlon Memorial Mosaic, San Francisco. (Photo by Corwin Hansen)

Mosaic has also been used to rehabilitate human beings. Therapeutic studies involving mosaic were led by instructors Bob Skiles and Gene Perrine in a project conducted by the Cherry Foundation for the young adults of the Cerebral Palsy Recreation Center in San Francisco. Therapy, an exercise to make muscles coordinate, and the creative act as exercised in crafts are two different things. However, it was felt that if these two things could be combined, the patients would benefit both physically and psychologically. Various mediums, such as ceramics, jewelry-making and painting, as well as mosaic, were explored for their therapeutic value. Of these, mosaic proved most interesting to these patients who since birth had been limited in co-ordination.

The project was introduced by a reading on mosaics, and slides of Byzantine mosaics were shown. Only one student had ever heard of mosaics before. Then each student chose a symbol which appealed to him, such as an arrow, a sun, a flower. Mosaic materials were brought, though no glass or material with sharp edges could be used. Pebbles, marbles, and homemade clay tiles were most successful. As the range of variation in the students' capability was so great, some of them even being in wheel chairs, it was decided to work on individual mosaics one foot square. The setting material for these mosaics was spackle. This mortar is easier to handle than sticky mastic or corrosive magnesite and cement.

From the start it was astonishing to see how these students, who co-ordinated with difficulty and often made many attempts at placing one tessera, could construct a mosaic. If a tessera was not placed exactly, it did not matter. Roughness in mosaic is desirable, and a pebble slightly out of line neither spoiled the work nor discouraged the student. The use of symbols, a method of communication in its simplest and most direct form, was also beneficial. Symbols provided an outlet for emotion in those whose speech was handicapped. A further psychological gain was accomplished when some of these students were able to make such articles as ash trays and plaques and their work was sold.

Mosaics were found to have excellent therapeutic value in the at-tempt to master control of fingers, hands and arms as a working combi-nation. Many hospitals might imitate this experiment. Centers where the handicapped are trained to become self-sufficient could find in mosaics a work both humanely and commercially profitable.

Immaculate Heart College, a liberal arts school of four hundred students conducted by Immaculate Heart of Mary religious in Los Angeles, might be called the mosaic center of western America. Several years ago the art department of this college instituted a class in mosaic which has grown so popular that additional day and night classes for adults and college students still cannot fill the demand of those wishing to make mosaics. Made under the sensitive direction of Sister Magdalen Mary and Sister Mary Corita, mosaics from this school have been exhibited throughout America, reproduced in national and international publications; and have been subjects of controversy, as many have refused to believe they could be the work of "students." The art department of Immaculate Heart College is itself frequently a subject of discussion. To jar students from clichés of seeing, thinking and drawing, Sister Magdalen Mary sometimes adopts surprising methods: students draw with chalk on the end of a long stick, or they outline simple forms with their eyes closed. Through such exercises, they enter into new worlds of form and color relation. The purpose of these methods and the department itself is not to achieve unrepresentational art for its own sake but to learn to see reality with fresh and creative eyes. Concerning the objectives of the Immaculate Heart Art Department, Sister Magdalen Mary says:

"We have not chosen a style. The so-called Immaculate Heart style is the result of our way of working. This way is opposed to repeating

FIGURE 50. Sister Magdalen Mary's mosaic class.

out of dead formulae the forms evolved in other eras. Such formulae were valid in their time and their organically-arrived-at forms are to be respected by us but not faked by us.

"Our way places emphasis on the necessity of appproaching problems unencumbered with preconceived notions no longer adequate in our time.

"We do not think our way is unreal. If realistic means apeing the effects of the real through inability to make contact with the real, then we are unrealistic."

A credo for today's art educators indeed! The work of Sister Magdalen Mary's students well illustrates the success of her aims.

FIGURE 51. Mosaic clock by Louisa Jenkins, at home of Mr. and
Mrs. George Rossi, Hillsborough, California.

13

Mosaic Design

A mosaic, like every man-made work, is only as good as its design. True, mosaic materials are in themselves beautiful. Yet no matter how intriguing these materials, their relationships when incorporated into a mosaic can be pleasing, inspiring, banal, or sterile. Design is the foundation upon which rests the character of every mosaic. Stones only repeat and emphasize this design; they are one of the many ways of illustrating it. Ancient Christians, for example, used to cover the walls of their churches with fresco. Later, as in Kahrie Djami, an old Byzantine church in Istanbul, they overlaid the frescos with mosaic because they wished to transform their designs into a more permanent material. Today, the character of design remains just as significant. A cartoon or finished drawing of a mosaic *is*, in a sense, the mosaic before tesserae are ever laid.

Timid people are likely to approach the subject of design with the protest, "But I've no talent for drawing and I'm practically color blind!" For these people, mosaic is a wonderful counter-protest. A mosaic design may be combined with something needed by every household—furniture. Suppose, for example, a coffee table is required. This table may be bought at a store or it may be designed especially for the home. If designed, the timid person has a foolproof method of construction. He can use a mosaic kit. These kits, found at hobby shops and art stores, supply a ready-made design and tesserae in just the right colors to fit this design. The timid person can obtain one of these kits, make a coffee table and gain confidence from this experience. He may discover, though, that the table does not fit precisely into his home. He will find himself tempted to try the spontaneity of his own design, and he should not be satisfied until he does. To follow a ready-made design develops confidence, but it also cheats the heart of any creative experience. The timid bird must be pushed from his nest so that, instead of watching, he may fly. Having once created an original

design, the timid person probably can never be persuaded to return
to the restrictions of a ready-made pattern.

Color selection for a mosaic can also be greatly simplified. Many
paint stores carry color charts, combinations of color worked out in
harmonious tones. Also, a good rule for fitting mosaic into a room is
to study the room itself. Pick out one color in the decor which might
be emphasized in mosaic. Use this color in all gradations from the
darkest to the lightest. Such a color scheme is known as monotone.
Monotone plus black and white provides an almost foolproof method
of fitting mosaic into a decor.

Simplicity, both in design and color, cannot be emphasized enough
when making a mosaic. There is something naive and childlike in the
very act of putting one stone next to another; the simplicity which
stems from this act should never be abandoned. When searching for
designs, remember to stress a *minimum* of colors and lines. There are

FIGURE 52. Pebble mosaic, patio, Louisa Jenkins.

dozens of ways to illustrate this rule. For instance, examine a magazine. The most arresting advertisements are always those where a few spots of color are arranged on an empty page. Notice the covers used for phonograph records. These are full of interesting colors and designs. Old pieces of handwoven material, the crude folk designs of early household utensils, all call attention to the basic simplicity of good design. Wall-papers, especially those with modern abstract patterns, may prove inspirational. Lastly, every library contains books on design with numerous illustrations. These books teach in principle what is everywhere obvious: the foundation of good design is simplicity (Figure 52).

Environment, the intimate day-to-day environment of each human being, is a mosaic of designs. Many people do not see them. The artist does. Yet this artist possesses no extraordinary vision. He has merely developed and organized the sensitive perception of his childhood. He wants to see, and so he is an artist—first of all—in the art of seeing. If he lives in the country, he will study nature. On a walk he will really look at the ground. He will stop to pick up leaves, stones with strange hieroglyphics etched on them and seeds with comical little faces. He will notice the wind and how it shifts the grasses to a rhythmic pattern. Moreover, as if this obvious world of nature were not enough, he will sometimes carry a magnifying glass. With it he will examine the design of the minutest spider web or some intricate lichens clinging to a rock. And suddenly, if he is a mosaicist, the artist will find the designs for his mosaics already made! They are everywhere around him. They are in the fresh-fallen leaves of autumn, in rocks along the seacoast, in the twining of seaweeds, in refuse cast by the water on the beach and riversides (Figure 53).

Artists who live in the city are no less aware of their surroundings. On rainy days there is light reflecting from dozens of puddles on the asphalt street, interplaying with those scraps of newspaper thrown into the gutter. What patterns! There is the junkyard with its innumer-

FIGURE 53. Mosaic designs in nature.

able treasures and designs waiting to be recognized. Old gears, the spring of a broken clock, rusty pans, all these can be used. Seeing the usually unobserved then becomes a game, a game of discovering the world as it exists about every person. Seeing is a matter of reality. Is this reality just a dish of melting ice cream that one couldn't finish, or is it a substance of strange mounds, swirls, pools of color running into each other, and through the glass dish a chequered tablecloth making a fascinating pattern? In his time, Leonardo da Vinci saw his own kind of ice cream. He said that one should look at walls stained with damp or at stones of uneven color, and one will be able to see in these the likeness of divine landscapes, adorned with mountains, rivers, rocks, woods, great plains, hills and valleys in great variety. He went on to tell how with the imagination one sees faces and battles in the same way. This was the vision of a genius, but to some extent it is possible to everyone. This same vision is a source of joy to children, and to most adults a lost faculty they could well reactivate.

Household objects, books, and environment, these three suggest mosaic designs, but there is another powerful source of design material. This is the symbol. Graphic symbols were a language used be-

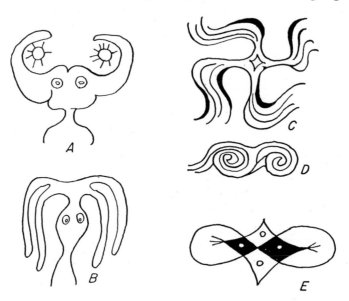

FIGURE 54. Spirals.
A, B. Octopus design from spiral. Palace of Knossus, Crete. *C, D.* Spirals. Knossus, Crete. *E.* South Sea Islands.

fore printing changed them into words and communication between
people became discursive. The direct impact of a graphic symbol has
been, to a great extent, lost. Symbols are especially important in
church design, but here it is enough to suggest that symbols are still
seen in signs of the zodiac, emblems of uniforms, flags, coins, and city
or national seals. Books on symbols, though rare, contain dozens of
these compelling designs (Figure 54).

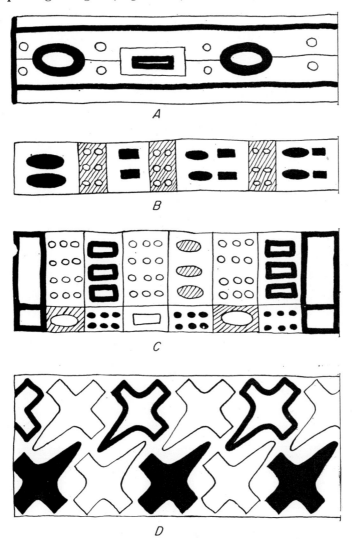

FIGURE 55. Border designs.

A, B, C. 7th Century Mosaics of Ravenna, Italy.

D. Contemporary border.

Having once selected a mosaic design, there is frequently a temptation to enlarge, embroider, and complicate it. To check this temptation, the artist should remember that he is going to work in blunt stones. A row of stones to replace a pencil line! Lines must consequently be kept broad. In drawing mosaic designs, it is best to use a piece of wide crayon or charcoal or a pen which makes a mark a quarter inch wide. With such tools the artist will be forced to think in basic masses and lines. Often, of course, a design is initiated by a thumbnail sketch which can be enlarged. But, when making a cartoon the same size as a mosaic, it is wise to draw lines a quarter inch wide for the tesserae which will ultimately replace them (Figure 55).

In many designs color is the most important factor. Colors are placed next to one another, contrasted, or made to flow together, and in this process the line between them sometimes disappears. When this type of mosaic is being designed, it is best to draw with a wide flat brush. Japanese paint brushes come in all sizes and are excellent for such a purpose. Large murals should be designed with a big brush; one four inches wide is not too extreme (Figure 56).

Since mosaic designs will be translated into stone, any durable quality of drawing paper and coloring material may be used. Wrapping paper, newsprint, or paper which has been used before will serve. Tracing paper is frequently needed for extra designs. A large roll of tracing paper is handy, and it may be bought at a draftsman's supply house.

An excellent way to draw a design for mosaic is by pinning a piece of paper to the studio wall. Draw with brush and show card colors or the dry colors used in kindergartens. Bold swirls of paint will result. Do not think of the cartoon as a painting or try for finished effects. This type of work can be painted over until a design has appeared or the paper has worn out. Another method of designing is to select one motif and repeat it in a variety of ways. Decorative repetition of geometric designs was incorporated by the ancient Romans into their floors and ceilings. Today these patterns can be used just as dramatically in floors and patios, but our civilization no longer decorates its ceilings. Could this be an indication of our gaze—down and never up? (Figure 57.)

The cartoon or finished drawing made by a mosaicist must always be drawn on heavy paper. This is especially true of large cartoons

FIGURE 56. Use of wide Japanese brush, studio of Louisa Jenkins.

where paper is cut into sections or where mosaic tesserae are laid directly on the paper and not embedded in cement. Butcher paper is best for cartoons. It can be divided into strips and taped together to form vast wall areas. After a cartoon is drawn, it should be colored before mosaic tesserae are selected.

A small drawing is frequently enlarged to form a cartoon. To enlarge tiny thumbnail sketches into good-sized drawings there is a tool called the pantograph. This tool is a combination of ruled, slotted, and jointed strips of wood. The drawing is tacked to a board, the pantograph adjusted, and a tracing made. This tracing appears on the drawing board enlarged; however, a pantograph will enlarge no more than several feet square.

FIGURE 57. Overall ceiling pattern, Oratorio di Santa Andrea, Ravenna, Italy.

When no enlarging machine is available, another method of expanding drawings is to rule the small sketch into squares. Then, using the same amount of squares but making them two or three times the size of the original squares, rule off the paper for the large cartoon. When this is done, follow the original drawing square by square until it is reproduced on the large-scale cartoon.

The best machine for enlarging is a projector. This machine, which throws a magnified image on the cartoon paper, greatly facilitates the enlarging process. A sketch is put into the enlarger and a magnified image of the sketch is cast upon the cartoon paper. This image is then traced. The amount of distance between machine and paper determines the size of an enlargement. An enlarging projector comes in several types and sizes and may be purchased at a camera store.

FIGURE 58. Cupola of Battistero, Florence.

14

Church Art

Whenever an Italian is questioned about mosaics, he will invariably refer to the art of the early Christian church. He will praise the church of Santa Constanza in Rome or rhapsodize about a certain eighth century wall in Ravenna. Speaking thus, he is not disparaging his own time but unconsciously pointing out the period when mosaic art was most alive. For mosaic, as used in churches during the Byzantine period, from the 5th to the 13th centuries, was not mere decoration but a kind of sacred cinema. Employing symbols and dramatic Biblical texts, its ultimate purpose was to raise the minds of its beholders to the contemplation of God. Medieval society was illiterate in our modern sense. No matter, mosaics explained the story. This art flourished before printing and spoke to society in a language all could understand— the language of graphic symbols. Like *Life* Magazine of today, mosaic carried pictorial headlines, only its "news" was different: The Creation

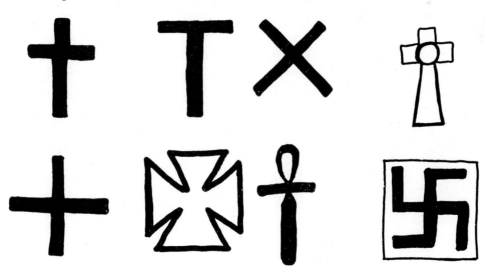

FIGURE 59. Variations of the Cross.

of Man, The Fall of Man, The Crucifixion of Christ, His Resurrection, and other sacred mysteries. Not only did mosaic carry "news," it also formed a link between the natural and supernatural worlds. Medieval society "read" these stories eagerly, while most people who can read words today are illiterate in the sense of graphic symbols (Figure 59).

There is no need to establish the value of Byzantine mosaics, which used symbols so effectively. These mosaics have existed for centuries as masterpieces, and in this age of comfortable travel some of them are the objects of arduous mule rides and hikes to isolated parts of the world where Byzantine culture once flourished. Nevertheless, the appreciation of Byzantine mosaics has been inconstant over the centuries. During the Victorian era, these mosaics were harshly criticized. Critics at that time could not value what seemed so foreign to them: stark patterns, rigid figures, and limited color range. It has taken an additional hundred years to reconcile this alienation. Twentieth century artists find something familiar in Byzantine work. Abstractionists particularly respect the Byzantine period. Perhaps this is because the modern artist, unlike his Victorian brother, is again seeking a message which will pierce to the *heart* of reality. He is desperate to communicate; perhaps he feels that twentieth century civilization has its back to the wall and there is little time. Whatever he feels, it is possible to see the Byzantine techniques of starkness and stylization echoing in many modern artists. Byzantines deliberately adopted these techniques to convey staggering truths which had no counterparts in nature, which could be told in no other way. For example, Mary, Mother of God, could not be merely a human being; therefore, the Byzantines did not depict her in conventional human form. In the same way, the modern artist searches for a means to communicate a reality he too finds staggering. His abstractions are not unrelated to those of the Byzantines, because both abstractions spring from the same source: a need to express significant and inner meanings. Neither Byzantine nor twentieth century artist is content to be occupied, as were the Victorians, with an elegant surface. (Figure 60.)

Byzantine church art, unlike twentieth century art in the church, is stylized. Whether in fresco, icons, illuminated manuscripts, or mosaics, Byzantine iconography remained the same. Its general composition and style rarely varied from a set pattern. Yet while objects such as the human body, animals, flowers, and trees are formal in the extreme, there is nothing static about this art. The work of the eighth

century especially has a primitive aliveness and violence. One is able
to see beyond the formalized figures to the essences they express. This
effect is curious, because it is thought by scholars of the Byzantine
period that many of these mosaics were not spontaneously designed.

FIGURE 60. Contemporary religious mosaic by Louisa Jenkins, St. Mary's
College, Indiana.

They were copies of illuminations from early Greek manuscripts. Miniatures were simply enlarged from a few inches of parchment to cover an entire facade. A comparison between certain mosaics and the illuminations from which they are thought to have been copied shows a great similarity of line and composition.

If Byzantine mosaics were not even freely designed, why do their compositions have anything in common with modern abstract art? Both arts deal with abstractions. There is no effort to present forms photographically. For instance, the Byzantines frequently made towers and walls of medieval cities on the same size and plane as figures of the saints. This effect was not, as Victorian critics supposed, a mistake. The Byzantine artist had a concept of perspective which is quite modern. His perspective was one in which lines do not converge or vanish in the distance but converge in the opposite direction and vanish in the eye of the beholder. Psychologically, the beholder's view is expanded to infinity and not constricted to a point (Figure 61).

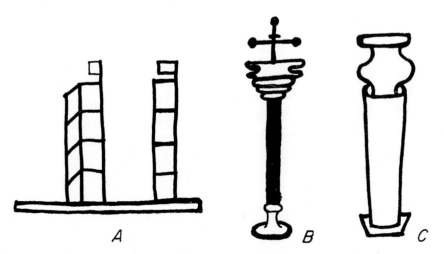

FIGURE 61. Column symbols.
A. Mayan. *B*. Christian. *C*. Palace of Knossus, Crete.

Ways of seeing change. After the Victorian era our way of seeing is again more closely allied to the Byzantine. Yet, powerful as these Byzantine mosaics are, they cannot be copied. Each age must speak in its own idiom. The twentieth century is not, of all things, Byzantine. Consequently the imitation Gothic churches still constructed today, with their imitation Byzantine mosaics, are sepulchres full of artistic corpses. They are sterile because they do not express the vital idiom of our times. This failure is curious. When modern art and architecture are incorporated so beautifully in public buildings, skyscrapers, factories and bridges, why must many of today's churches mumble only of the past? Since when has the artist's eye been bound to the past? Frequently the failure of religious art is due in part to clergy or officials, who are given architectural control of a church and whose knowledge of art has stopped with the Gothic or mid-Victorian. Such people have not had time to investigate the new vision that the artist of today is trying to portray. Until there is cooperation and exchange of ideas among clergy, architect, and artist, there will be few good examples of present-day creative spirit in religious buildings.

What is the difference between religious and secular art? Essentially these two arts are one. In both cases the artist is a mediator. However, in secular art it is nature, the obvious, the commonplace, the so-called still life or landscape that the artist tries to interpret. He attempts to pierce through the surface of a natural object in order to recreate its essence, hoping the beholder in turn will catch a little of the mystery and wonder of life around him. Religious art also has this purpose. However, in religious art the artist is mediator between the truths of a Faith and its followers. Pope Pius XII clearly defined the purpose of religious art when he stated: "The function of art is to break the agonizing circle of the finite in which man is enclosed in this life and to open a window of his mind for the Infinite."

In America, where tradition does not weigh heavily as it does in Europe, experimentation and fresh design in mosaics should be and are being encouraged. When it comes to church art, the most logical place for mosaics to be made is in a group dedicated to religious life itself. One such group, the Benedictine monks at Mount Angel Abbey, Oregon, has a mosaic studio. With a long heritage of artistic appreciation in Gregorian chant and music, these monks recognized the beauty of mosaics and asked permission to make them. A room in the monastery basement was cleared and scrubbed, a few tools were requisitioned, and scrap material was donated by local glass and tile studios. Then a class in mosaic began. Each monk devoted what little spare time he had to constructing mosaics. Groups of young seminarians came to see the work and, when time permitted, participated in it. A carpentry shop on the monastery grounds supplied whatever framing material

and installation were needed. Today the Benedictine monks at Mount
Angel have more than an art class. They are producing mosaics to
decorate their own and other buildings. These mosaics have also been
exhibited in the United States and are in keeping with the tradition of
the Benedictine Order—an interest in art which is not of the past but
a living force.

FIGURE 62. Mosaic class, Mt. Angel Monastery, Oregon.

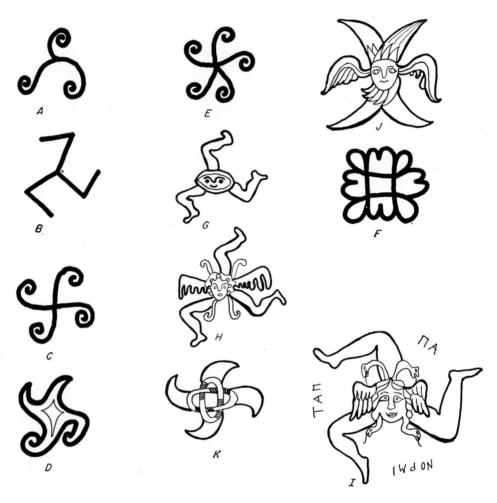

FIGURE 63. *A, B.* Triskelion, three-armed. *C, D.* Tetraskelion, four-armed. *E.* Spiral or volute. *F.* Mosaic pattern on floor, from Rhodes. *G, H, I.* Variations of Triskelion. *J, K.* Variations of Tetraskelion.

15

Symbols

A symbol is the best possible representation of an unknown fact. This representation may be a myth, a ritual, or a drawing. Because symbols stand for the unknown, their definitions are as varied as the authors who try to explain them. However, when related to mosaics, symbols are a language developed by the artist to convey an idea to the beholder directly. In this sense, the use of symbols reached its peak in the western world during medieval times. This was no accident. Since artists of that period were communicating mysteries which transcended nature and could not be explained by material means, they used symbols.

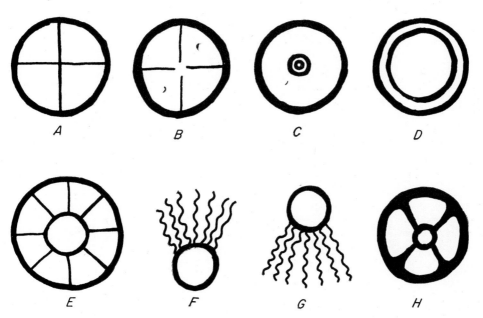

FIGURE 64. Circle and sun symbols. *A, B, C, D.* Sun symbols, 13th Century Mosaics, Ravenna, Italy. *E.* North American Indian. *F.* Rising sun, North American Indian. *G.* Setting sun, North American Indian. *H.* Mexican.

101

Undoubtedly, the problem of conveying the unknown by means of symbols is as old as human society. Witness the marks carved into rock caves by prehistoric man throughout the world. The study of symbols has always interested scholars and they have accumulated vast data on this subject. From these data a curious fact emerges. Certain basic forms seem to have attracted man and remained significant during all ages and cultures. Such forms as the cross, square, circle—with different interpretations—have been repeated since the beginning of man (Figure 64).

But, the mosaicist may ask, what have symbols to do with my work? A great deal. Artists have always been carriers not only of beauty, culture, and ideas but of the symbols expressing these ideas, and so by using the language of symbolism they have in a sense interpreted man to himself. Every age has produced artists to express its goals and

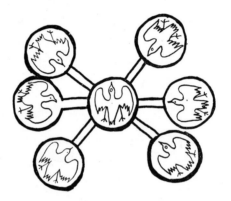

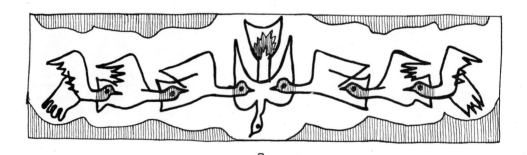

B

FIGURE 65. Seven gifts of the Holy Spirit. *A*. Window of Abbey St. Dennis. 12th century. *B*. Contemporary mosaic, by Louisa Jenkins.

values. When, as in mosaic, such goals and values are depicted symbolically, the mosaicist has served to perpetuate these basic symbols.

But man's conception of the unknown changes. Each age must speak for itself and no two ages are alike. Today, artists who deal with symbols in church art often feel that a symbol expressed traditionally is a symbol expressed best. Yet, for instance, the symbol of the bird, showing in medieval times the seven gifts of the Holy Spirit, will be quite different as seen through the eyes of the present day artist (Figure 65).

Sometimes, too, the artist has little experienced the vital impact of the relationship between symbol and what is symbolized. Without this experience, the symbol he draws has no power. Medieval artists knew and loved symbols and the realities they expressed. Consequently, when these artists used a symbol, it reflected the depth of their knowledge and love. Today, however, symbols are all too often copied from books. Such symbols have the blessings of tradition, they are pleasant designs, but, as copies, they are made without knowledge or love. They are then like mummies dragged up from other ages, lifeless images which can be imitated but not revivified.

Twentieth century society does not think much about symbols. Books written within the last hundred years describe symbols as a "lost" language. Fortunately abstract artists are once again discovering the power of symbols and there is renewed interest in the subject, though the bulk of society is not yet concerned. Why not? To begin with, the use of symbols as a language declined when printing was invented. Society became literate and familiar with discursive communication. No longer was it necessary to present an idea graphically when it could be developed and explained in detail by the printed page. Printing having been perfected, a fullness of explanation was gained but something important was lost. People stopped visualizing in terms of symbols and communication lost much of its direct impact. Ideas were no longer grasped instantly or intuitively as a single unit but understood piece by piece in an orderly sequence of thought. Simultaneously with this profound change in thought, another change took place in society. Gradually values were shifted from the intangible to the tangible, from the spiritual to the material world. Any unknown which could not ultimately be reduced to physical elements or proved according to the material laws of the universe became spurious, an impossibility not worth the trouble of serious consideration. What man could

not explain, was not: such became the philosophy of the "new thinker."
Perhaps it might be said that man lost his intellectual humility, his
ability to regard anything which transcended natural law as valuable
—in short, his ability to be confronted with and to contemplate a mystery. Recognizing no unknown facts to contemplate, there was no
need to represent these facts. Symbols were struck a death blow before
they could be born (Figure 66).

FIGURE 66. Designs on circle. *A*. French Tarot card,
19th century. *B*. Monogram of Christ—St. Vitale, 6th
century, Ravenna, Italy. *C, D*. Mississippi Indian.

Because modern man has ceased to act upon, to fill and fulfill his
life with mysteries, it is possible to say that the language of symbols
has declined. No longer do symbols lead in church art, where once
they were most powerful. Speaking more widely, symbols, from conveying a message of the supernatural, have been perverted into signs
representing the material goods toward which twentieth century man
races to satisfy his spiritual starvation. The difference between a symbol and a sign is this: Symbols relate to the unknown, signs to the

known. An example of the degeneration of symbols into signs is the symbol of three interlocking circles. Once this form represented the Tri-une God of Christianity. Now it has come to signify the trade-name of a beer!

This view of symbols might be depressing were it not for one fact: having endured through the history of mankind, symbols seem likely to be as permanent as man himself, only waiting to be rediscovered as man rediscovers his spiritual needs. With the renewed interest in religion evident in the middle of the twentieth century, it is perhaps accurate to speak of symbols as a language which is being rediscovered. Moreover, new symbols are continually being created. They are formed as the experiences and boundaries of mankind are enlarged. Just as new words are coined to keep up with the enlarged vision of man, so new symbols come into use. For example, who knows if the world of man's flight into the air is not endowing the airplane with the power to express the life of the firmament? Or how about the terror and destructive force associated with that mushroom form peculiar to an exploding hydrogen bomb? And what new symbols will be born from the world being explored in the ocean? Man knows little of this world as yet, but as science probes deeper and deeper, more and more of the world underwater will be revealed, even as sportsmen skin divers now explore the shallows. Such knowledge cannot be without symbolic fruit.

The mosaic artist has a particular obligation to investigate the language of symbols. More and more frequently his work appears in public places; and mosaic has always had a prominent place in church art, where symbols are in a sense the heartbeat of good design and communication. Mosaic, furthermore, being the most permanent of arts, will have spectators spanning many generations. And finally, because of the way mosaics are constructed, their simplicity of stone or glass can best expound the simple direct forms of basic symbols.

In these few paragraphs, it has been impossible to do more than suggest the existence and the value of symbols. Nothing has been conveyed of the richness of specific symbols, though many fascinating books have been written on this subject. A selection of these books appears in the bibliography at the back of this book. The two-volume edition of THE LOST LANGUAGE OF SYMBOLISM, by Harold Bayley, may be recommended at once and should be in the library of every mosaicist.

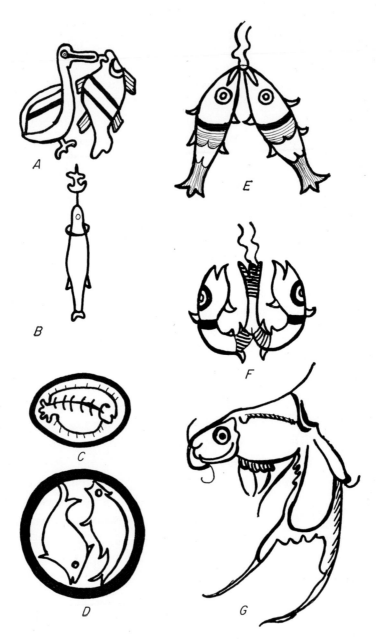

FIGURE 67. Fish symbols. *A.* Mayan. *B.* Catacombs, Rome. *C.* Fish in solar eye. *D.* Fish of zodiac in floor of Battistero, Florence. *E, F.* Fish as Alpha-Omega, Vatican Library manuscript. *G.* Contemporary Chinese plate design.

16

People and Projects

This chapter lists, alphabetically, only a few of the many fine artists in mosaic of today who are experimenting with new techniques and whose work is now beautifying public buildings, churches, and private homes and gardens.

Jean and Arthur Ames. These artists, of Claremont, California, have designed and executed an altar in glass mosaic for the Claremont Community Church, in gold on a red ground, with white and silver (Figures 68).

Mary Bowling, who is of half-Korean, half Scotch-Irish descent, designs murals with a highly imaginative charm and fantasy, some of which now adorn buildings in Los Angeles, Palm Springs, and the Beverly-Hilton Hotel in Beverly Hills. She calls the products of her particular technique *Intarsias* (Figure 69).

Ada Bethune is known mostly for her religious art work, including large mosaics for churches in the Philippine Islands and in Mexico. In constructing these mosaics she has used the help of the native people. She has often worked with the simplest of materials, such as broken colored bottles in place of colored glass, producing outstanding effects (Figure 70).

Helen Bruton and *Jeanne Reynal* were the first to introduce contemporary mosaic in the United States. Before the war, Helen Bruton, with her sisters, Margaret Bruton and Esther Gilman, had mosaic projects at the Fleishhacker Playground in San Francisco and at the university of California in Berkeley. Since then she has executed many large murals, including several for the Matson Line, the Thomas Starr King School in San Francisco, and St. Joseph's College in Mountain View. She has experimented with many different ways of laying mosaic, the latest of which is the using of an electric router to let in design areas in

FIGURE 68. Glass mosaic by Jean and Arthur Ames, Claremont Community Church, Claremont, California.

FIGURE 69. Detail of mural by Mary Bowling, Beverly-Hilton Hotel, Beverly Hills, California.

FIGURE 70. Mural mosaic by Ade Bethune, St. Joseph's Church, Victorias Milling Co., Philippine Islands.

panels of wood. The mosaic is then glued into these areas with poly-vinal resin glue. (Figures 71 and 72.)

Dorothy Puccinelli Cravath, of Berkeley, California, is known primarily for her beautiful murals of pebble mosaic, though she has recently executed a mosaic church façade using other materials. (Figures 73 and 74.)

FIGURE 71. Helen Bruton preparing mosaic
materials.

FIGURE 72. Mosaic by Helen Bruton.

FIGURE 74. Church façade by Dorothy Cravath.

FIGURE 73. Pebble mosaic cross by Dorothy Cravath.

Richard Haines, also a well-known painter and now on the faculty of the Los Angeles County Art Institute, has executed mosaic murals in many public buildings, including the new Music Building at the University of California at Los Angeles. (Figure 75.)

FIGURE 75. Detail of mosaic by Richard Haines, Music Building, University of California at Los Angeles.

Louisa Jenkins started her work with mosaic when she was making collages which included glass. Her first mosaic show was in San Francisco in 1947. Since then she has experimented in many techniques, working on religious subjects as well as with mosaic murals for public buildings and private homes. Her show in New York in 1953 illustrated many of the interesting results of these experimentations. (Figures 76, 77, 78 and 79.)

FIGURE 77. Mosaic of St. Teresa of Avila, in study of Louisa Jenkins, Big Sur, California.

FIGURE 76. Part of mosaic altarpiece (Triptych) by Louisa Jenkins, Mt. La Salle Novitiate Chapel, Christian Brothers, Napa, California.

FIGURE 79. Relief mosaic, head of Christ, by Louisa Jenkins.

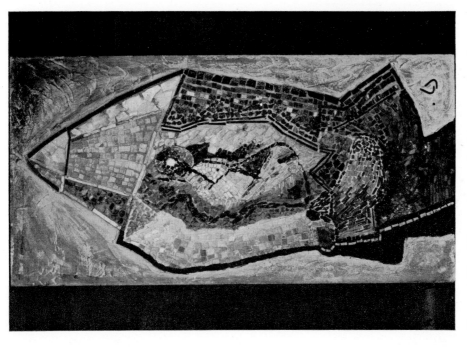

FIGURE 78. Magnesite and glass mosaic, abstract form, by Louisa Jenkins.

Jeanne Reynal, presently of New York City, has spent years of arduous experiment in mosaic, after working under Boris Aurep in Paris. She has traveled far from traditional bonds and has been widely exhibited. Her approach to mosaic can best be expressed by quoting from a letter of hers on this subject:

> "Though I have deviated from the line and made some excursions in color, I think that the use of line over colored areas will remain my first interest. I harp always on the theme of "breath" in the working of stones; so I suppose the line and space, the air around each stone, are my main preoccupations."

(Figures 80 and 81)

FIGURE 80. Jeanne Reynal in studio.

FIGURE 81. Mosaic by Jeanne Reynal.

FIGURE 82. Detail of fresco mosaic, "Tree of Jesse" by Elsa Schmid,
Chapel, Yale University.

Elsa Schmid is noted for her religious murals, in which she has combined, in a most original way, her own use of fresco and mosaic. Her studio is in Rye, New York. (Figure 82.)

Max Spivak, whose studio is at 175 Madison Ave., New York, has done mosaic murals for public buildings in the east and in Los Angeles, as well as for the *S.S. Constitution* and *S.S. Independence*, of the American Export Lines. (Figure 83.)

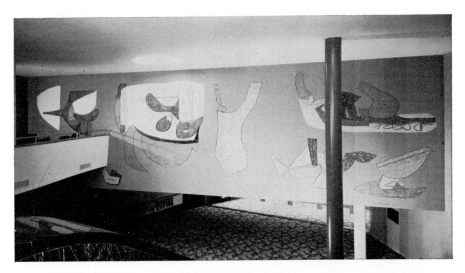

FIGURE 83. Mosaic mural by Max Spivak, Calderone Theatre, Hempstead, New York.

Joseph Young, although still in his thirties, has already executed many large mosaic murals. His studio is in Los Angeles, where he has settled after studies in Rome. Photographs of the working procedures of his studio are used to illustrate techniques described in Chapter IX of this book. (Figure 84.)

FIGURE 84. Mosaic mural by Joseph Young, Temple Emanuel, Beverly Hills, California.

THE NATIONAL UNIVERSITY OF MEXICO

The exterior mosaic, by *Juan O'Gorman*, which covers ten floors of the Library of the National University in Mexico City, was completed in 1953 (Figure 85). This was the first monumental contemporary mosaic to be done on this continent and it caused widespread interest among architects and artists alike. It brought to the attention of our architects, as nothing else has done, the possibilities of decoration and so started much designing and planning along these lines in the United States.

FIGURE 85. Exterior mosaic of Library of National University of Mexico.

This mosaic extends over 4,400 square feet and is composed of natural stone. The subject matter of one wall relates to the pre-Hispanic eras and depicts Aztec ceremonies and symbols. Another wall pictures events of the colonial times. Since the artist-designer of the mosaic and the co-architect of this building are one and the same person, the result is one of outstanding integrity and beauty.

Construction

First a number of small-sized black and white drawings were made by Mr. O'Gorman; then color sketches. After these were completed the full-sized cartoons were done with the aid of assistants, since the area to cover was immense. A drawing wall of 135′ x 20′ was constructed and paper tacked to it. On this the cartoons were done in reverse. The colors to be used, being uncomplicated, were merely indicated in writing. Then these cartoons were cut in meter squares, which were laid on the floor, face up, in plaster frames. On these the workmen laid the stones, which were roughly 1½″ to 2″ in diameter. An inch of concrete was poured over the stones and steel hooks embedded. Then, after the concrete had hardened, the squares were lifted and the paper peeled away; 3,700 sections were made in this way and numbered. The wall on which the mosaic was to be installed had had a mesh of steel rods embedded in it. The workmen then lifted the sections of mosaic, one by one, and hung them on the steel rods, cementing them in place.

The tesserae of which this beautiful mosaic is composed were made from rocks of ten different colors. When the finished work had been scrubbed and cleaned, the surface was weather-proofed. The project took a year to complete.

Mosaic Supplies: Where to Find Them

Tools, adhesives, and tesserae for mosaic may be purchased in many large cities throughout America, but a beginner in this art often wonders just how to find them. Art stores do not always stock mosaic materials. Nevertheless, an increasing number of art shops are selling mosaic materials as the medium becomes more popular.

Bibliography

Symbolism

The Lost Language of Symbolism—Harold Bayley. 2 Vol. J. B. Lippincott Co. 1913

Symbols and Emblems of Early and Mediaeval Christian Art—Louisa Twining. Longman, Brown, Green & Longmans. 1852

Symbolism in Christian Art—F. Edward Hulme. Macmillan Co., New York. 1910

American Antiquities of the Red Race—Alexander W. Bradford. Dayton & Saxton. 1841

The Swastika—Thomas Wilson. Smithsonian Institution. Government Printing Office. 1896

The Tarot of the Bohemians—Papus. Chapman & Hall, Ltd. London. 1892

Mosaics

Art in the Early Church—Walter Lowrie. Pantheon Books. 1947

Mosaici Antichi di San Marco a Venezia—Sergio Bettini. Instituto Italiano D'Arti Grafiche. Bergamo

The Mosaics of Antioch—C. R. Morey. Longmans, Green & Co., New York. 1938

The Mosaics of Haghia Sophia at Istanbul—Thomas Whittemore. The Byzantine Institute. Vol. 2, 3, 4. Oxford University Press, London

Religious Art—Emile Male. Pantheon Books. 1949

The books which are listed below contain some information on the technique of mosaic.

A History of Mosaics—Edgar W. Anthony. Porter Sargent, Boston. 1935. Chap. 2.

La Mosaique—Adrien Blanchet. Payot, Paris. 1928. Chap. 1.

East Christian Art; A Survey of the Monuments—O. M. Dalton. Clarendon Press, Oxford. 1925. Pp. 266-298.

Leadless Decorative Tiles, Faience and Mosaic—W. J. Furnival. W. J. Furnival, Staffordshire, Eng. 1904. Vol. 2.

Mosaic and Allied Techniques—Albert H. King. Southern California W.P.A. Art Project. 1940

Mural or Monumental Decoration: Its Aims and Methods—W. Cave Thomas. Winsor and Newton, London. 1869. Pp. 74-105

Vasari on Technique—Giorgio Vasari. Translated by Louisa S. Maclehose. J. M. Dent & Co., London. 1907. Includes several chapters on technique of mosaics.

Design

Vision in Motion—L. Moholy-Nagy. Paul Theobald, Chicago.

Language of Vision—Gyorgy Kepes. Paul Theobald, Chicago.

Folk Art of Rural Pennsylvania—Frances Lichten. Charles Scribner's Sons, New York. 1946

Design From Peasant Art—Kathleen Mann. Adam & Charles Black, London. 1939

Index